T0148054

WHEN WOMEN FIRST WORE ARMY SHOES

A FIRST-PERSON ACCOUNT OF SERVICE AS A MEMBER
OF THE WOMEN'S ARMY CORPS DURING WWII.

ETHEL A. STARBIRD

iUniverse, Inc.
New York   Bloomington

This narrative is previously un-published but partially distributed as an undated typescript to Ethel A. Starbird's family under the title "Grandmother Wore Army Shoes" around 1999.

Edited by Susan Starbird Stout and Victoria Selfridge, Ethel A. Starbird's niece and grand-niece.

Photos in this publication are from the personal scrapbooks of Ethel A. Starbird and are presumed to be government photos in the public domain unless otherwise noted. iUniverse books may be ordered through booksellers or by contacting:

iUniverse
1663 Liberty Drive
Bloomington, IN 47403
www.iuniverse.com
1-800-Authors (1-800-288-4677)

ISBN: 978-1-4502-0893-2 (sc)
ISBN: 978-1-4502-0896-3 (ebook)

Library of Congress Control Number: 2010921958

Printed in the United States of America

iUniverse rev. date: 03/18/2010

Acknowledgments

The publication of this book wouldn't have been possible without the support of "the nieces and nephews:" Catharine Starbird Dalton, Beth (Bethie) Dalton Snyder, Emily W. Jennison, Colonel Edward A. Starbird, Susan Starbird Stout, and Catharine Ward.

Edited with love and affection
for our fearless and feisty
"Auntie Babe."
- Susan Starbird Stout & Victoria Selfridge

Contents

Foreword

WHAT FOLLOWS is intended as a light-hearted remembrance of how American women, as represented by the writer, acquitted themselves in their first mass encounter with military service. The time was World War II and participants in this unprecedented experiment were known during most of their existence as WACs – members of the Women's Army Corps.

As makers of history, they may not rank up there with Molly Pitcher but their successors, now meeting the ever more rigorous demands of modern-day soldiering, probably would not be where they are today if we had not been where we were then. Nor would this new generation and gender of GI be looking forward with some optimism to calling a future Chief of Staff "m'am" if some of their grandmothers hadn't worn Army shoes.

The WAC's early success was largely due to its first Director (1942-45), an accomplished Texan named Oveta Culp Hobby who faced prejudice, indifference, and even downright hostility to achieve acceptance for the Corps, which at peak strength in April 1945 numbered just under 100,000.

Sworn into the Women's Army Auxiliary Corps as a virtual Colonel (with a Major's pay), Hobby became an actual Colonel (with commensurate salary) when the Corps was absorbed into the Army over a year later. By law, neither she nor any other

WAC could ever rise higher. The male military did a bit better for themselves: they rated at least three General officers for every 12,000 men.

By the time the WAC was demobilized in 1978, enrollment had dropped to 53,000 and the Army had had a slight change of heart: all three Directors after 1970 wore Brigadier General's stars. Yet, in 1979, when I petitioned the Texas delegation in Congress to retroactively award Mrs. Hobby equivalent rank – which would involve no compensation since she could claim neither retired nor reserve status, only Lloyd Bensen responded favorably.

Stories like those assembled here often rely on lovingly-preserved letters, artifacts unearthed in some attic, or that more recent and provocative source: "previously sealed documents." Alas, of these I have none except a few ratty copies of my orders from my 201 file and, defying all logic, the rusted knife from my mess kit.

Instead, I have depended for material almost entirely on my somewhat shopworn remember-ability and that of a few hardy souls with whom I served. For WAC affairs in general during those early years, I am deeply indebted to Lt. Col. Mattie E. Treadwell for her masterful history of the WAAC/WAC – *The Women's Army Corps* – published in 1954 by the Department of the Army.

That Treadwell and I plow some of the same furrows in our separate accounts is understandable; much of her coverage of WAC activities in the Southwest Pacific originated with observations regularly reported to Hobby's headquarters from 1st Lt. Velma P. Griffith[1]. Since "Pat" was my boss and I her only

---

1   As noted in Treadwell's bibliographical notes for *The Women's Army Corps*, "No official history of the WAC in the Southwest Pacific theater has been written. Because of differences of opinion in the records, research has been carried to the unit records level, although time and facilities did not permit this to be done for other theaters. Besides thirty folders of theater files now at Field Records Division, Kansas City Records Center, Kansas City, Mo., the account of the WAC in the Southwest Pacific is based on the following reports: (1) The *"Griffith Account,"* an unsigned, undated typescript presented to the author by the War Department Bureau of Public Relations. Authorship of this document is reliably attributed to Capt. Velma P. Griffith, WAC Public Relations Officer, Southwest Pacific Area, who was an eyewitness to many events described therein, and who had access to theater WAC data. It is in agreement with other accounts and offers

"troop," much of the information footnoted to her derived from our shared experience.

The terms WAAC and WAC are used here within their proper time frames: WAAC for the period from May 14, 1942 when Congress' enabling act became law, to September 1, 1943; the WAC designation applies from that date when the "Auxiliary" was dropped until 1978 when women were finally and fully integrated into the United States Army.

Although this is largely a one-woman narrative, it is generously interspersed with background information about the wartime WAC that should make its story more understandable to those not fortunate enough to have lived it. And don't expect any two of us to recollect alike: despite an inescapable sameness in military diet, dress, and daily duties, every WAC's experience was uniquely her own.

All individuals mentioned here did exist and the events related to them did occur, no matter how fanciful some may now seem. Not everyone was known by the names I have used, their real ones having been lost in the tunnel of time. So I've taken the liberty of rechristening some on a purely fictional basis; any resemblance between these pseudonyms and actual persons living or dead is purely intentional.

Having spent the last twenty-three years of my work life with a magazine where accuracy was absolute, hard facts in this account have been verified to the extent possible after so many years. Any errors that may have survived are unintended and regretted.

As for the personal parts of this account, I figured one WAC's recall after more than a half-century is about as reliable as the next. This is mine.

— Ethel Starbird

---

a valuable narrative of experiences of WAC detachments, although not employed as an authority for statistics or policy."

One

I Want to Join the Army

MY FATHER was a very remarkable fellow. He could wriggle his ears singly or in unison, blow perfect smoke rings one inside the other, and peel an entire apple with one unbroken spiral of skin. Combining a prodigious memory with something he called "Maine logic" – only because he came from there – he could win, at least in his own view, almost every dinner-table debate that erupted on my regular Sunday visits to my parent's Vermont farm on the sunset side of Mount Mansfield.

He was having trouble with this one.

"You want to join the **what**?"

"Not the *what*, Dad – the WAAC – the Women's Army Auxiliary Corps."

"Dear God," groaned my father, "you can't be serious. Every time a car backfires you and the dog dive under the bed; your mother hasn't had to dust there in years. That would seem to indicate that you're not the warrior type."

"Alfred, don't be so profane," my mother scolded. "If I were thirty years younger that's exactly where I'd be."

"Not without a divorce you wouldn't."

Had the conversation continued in this vein, I was pretty sure the meal would cool off before my father did. So I decided not to mention at that time – early spring of 1943 – that I had already made two unsuccessful trips to the recruiting office only to be

1

rejected for the most absurd of reasons: I was simply too skinny. (Although every bit as porky as today's high-fashion models.)

My mother would have been cheered by the news, had I told her. With her only son and son-in-law (both proportionately as thin as I) already overseas, she had no sympathy with slackers and presumed everyone else felt the same way – until she ran into Mrs. Barber in the village store. Knowing the woman had a draft-age son, she asked where he was and what he was doing.

"Oh," said Mrs. B, "he's a C.O. out in Colorado."

My mother couldn't have been more effusive. "How proud you must be; so young and already a C.O.…."

Passing on this bit of neighborhood news to the postmistress a few days later, mother learned to her mortification that C.O., which as an Army brat she knew only as Commanding Officer, meant, in this case, conscientious objector. Not on mother's ball team at all. I really believe she thought it her patriotic duty to compensate for the Barber drop-out by offering up another of her own and, in these trying times, even a daughter would do. But given the hopeless state of my weight or lack thereof, it seemed doubtful she would ever sew another star on the family's service flag.

Meanwhile the WAAC was having troubles of its own.

Ram-rodded through Congress by a determined Massachusetts Representative named Edith Nourse Rogers, this first of the women's World War II military services had been born on May 14, 1942 amid confusion in the delivery room, protracted labor pains, and a far from unanimous approval rating.

During House debate on enabling legislation, Congressman Hoffman of Michigan, rising in opposition, delivered this zinger: "Take the women into the armed services in any appreciable numbers, who then will manage the home fires, who will do the cooking, the washing, the mending, the humble, homey tasks to which every woman has devoted herself?" Other anti-arguments: enlistment would deplete the dwindling supply of domestic help; a woman's army would offend America's manhood. Once on the floor, the bill passed handily.

The Navy, having already blueprinted a similar organization, wisely waited in the wings to see if the WAAC would fall on its face. When it didn't, the WAVES emerged wearing a far snappier uniform and a much niftier name; coined without the burden of literal translation – it meant Women Accepted for Voluntary Emergency Service – this apt acronym could not be corrupted as WAAC soon was to "wacky" and "wacko."

Once in business, the Corps acquired its initial strength by militarizing civilian women already working as filter board operators for the Aircraft Warning Service. They, like those who followed, entered as volunteer "auxiliaries" with the Army but not of it, doing as important support jobs as any other soldier but lacking almost all of his benefits. This non-status status, which subsequent services managed to escape, further complicated the WAAC's first year.

To guide all this pioneering woman power in an alien, monochromatic world, Pentagon officials – with a considerable push from Chief of Staff George Marshall – had chosen a soft-spoken, high-voltage Texan named Oveta Culp Hobby as the Corps' first Director. An experienced lawyer, editor, publisher, and civic leader, Hobby who as a civilian had helped Marshall shape early WAAC plans was already familiar with the pressure cooker wartime Washington had become.

Despite her impressive *curriculum vitae*, a noticeable reluctance arose among later planning officers, then available only in one gender, to yield authority to a newly minted Colonel (paid as a Major) of the opposite sex. They could not concede that being a woman – at which Hobby had excelled for some 38 years – could possibly give her any particular insight into running an organization consisting entirely of women.

As a consequence, many major decisions came entirely from a band of brothers whose association with females in the military was limited to an occasional Army nurse and fading memories of mares on the stable line. They, not Hobby, would provide much of the early misdirection on how the WAAC would be fed, trained, clothed, and utilized.

But before the results of their combined wisdom could reach the field (a term applied to just about anywhere outside a training center) local commanders were ordered to start processing candidates for the first officers' class due to report to Ft. Des

Moines, Iowa, on July 20, 1942. Lacking sex-specific instructions, some felt the rules that already regulated almost every aspect of Army life were plenty good enough for the women – and acted accordingly.

Which is why I - one of the original 30,000 to apply - never even made the first cut. For, by the only weigh-in chart then recognized – one designed exclusively for men – I was an unacceptable 33 pounds below the number required for my age (25) and height (5′7 ½″).

The authorities had, however, made one concession: the bend-over-and-cough routine for the men had been replaced with a back-down-legs-up position for the ladies. In more civilized society, this indignity is reserved until the end of a physical exam, not the first; any earlier disqualification eliminates the need for such intimacies.

Not at the station hospital at nearby Ft. Ethan Allen, scene of my several check-ups and let-downs. Here, the pelvic preceded the weigh-in, causing me unnecessary trips to the stirrup table. Perhaps the reason Ethan Allen medicos insisted on this progression was because the post had recently been reactivated for transient troops traveling without dependants; WAAC hopefuls were about the only women who passed that way and the doctors were determined to make the most of their opportunities.

By early summer, I had taken and failed the entrance exam yet a third time, never reaching the standard 143 pounds or the 15 pounds below it allowable on waiver. I've passed both since – and it's not a pretty sight.

Because rationing had already imposed certain restraints on human consumption, there was little hope that I would make up this deficit in the foreseeable future.

Imbued with the spirit of selflessness this particular war inspired, I signed up for a course in motor mechanics, volunteered my aging "woody" station wagon as an emergency ambulance, had its balding tires recapped with rubber soles from Sikora's Repair Shop, painted my legs an indifferent shade of beige to simulate non-replaceable silk hose, and learned to drink – with sometimes disastrous results – any old brand of anything the state liquor store happened to have in stock.

I was finally accepting the impossibility of my ever becoming a petticoat panzer.

Along about this time, the WAAC itself underwent a mighty change: shedding auxiliary status with its restraints, it became the Women's Army Corps – the WAC – a full-fledged component of the Army of the United States with pay and privileges equal to those of their brothers-in-arms – which Hobby had advocated from the very start.

The previous year had been a rough one for her and the WAAC. Trapped in a maze of conflicting policies and unclear command systems, Hobby & Co. coped with a degree of discrimination beyond the comprehension of later generations. Plagued with shortages of just about everything, early enrollees shivered through that first Iowa winter in outsized GI-issue overcoats, galoshes, caps, and gloves looking more like Napoleon's retreat from Moscow than the crisply-uniformed poster girls they expected to resemble. The only WAAC items then available for distribution: a floppy fatigue hat, "L'il Abner" field boots, and a shapeless seersucker number Cinderella would spurn.

Fluctuating recruitment goals delayed suppliers and scuttled future plans before they even rolled off the mimeograph machine. Temporary solutions to the space problem, like turning over three partially occupied prisoner-of-war camps in Louisiana for additional training centers, kicked up such bad press and parental alarm that recruiting slowed to a creep – just as demand for WAAC know-how was beginning to escalate. All of this while a campaign of slander, much of it generated by male soldiers who had never seen a WAAC, took its toll on the enlistment effort.

Then came the Corps' very own Contra affair – the contraceptive contretemps....

It started, more or less, when a high level meeting, to which no WAAC was invited, proposed issuing prophylactics and contraceptives to all auxiliaries. Plainly, such a plan, in a period of lukewarm public support, could scuttle the entire Corps.

Hobby, incensed and gutsy enough to skip channels (a military no-no), convinced the Deputy Chief of Staff to quash any such idea. She considered the subject closed.

The WAAC itself was well aware that pregnancy, elective

or otherwise, could become a serious occupational hazard; that prompt detection would benefit all concerned – since motherhood of minor children was forbidden in the service. Corps' staff proposed a viable early warning system: that the rabbit test be made available at all appropriate installations. It went nowhere, the opposition claiming that, given the habit of rabbits, assembling and maintaining that many celibate coneys would place an unnecessary strain on the war effort.

Concern for the WAAC's sex life reached a headline high in mid-1943 when a syndicated columnist named O'Donnell charged that skirted soldiers, like the trousered type, would be issued contraceptives. Denunciation of the entire Corps thundered from press to pulpit. Despite denials from the President on down, it began to look like the WAAC would expire before it was much more than a year old.

(Nor was this the end of the matter. As the war wound down, a carload of contraceptive jelly turned up for sale as Army Surplus. Naturally, no one would admit responsibility for the purchase; it probably fell on some well-meaning subaltern applying a too-literal translation to the phrase "or equivalent equipment.")

About this time, the recruitment bubble burst. Saddled with unrealistic quotas and a pool of eligibles drained by war industries and civil service, both with higher priority, the inevitable happened: a lowering of standards for selection.

Even the size of the existing Corps was shrinking for under the rules of the WAAC-to-WAC transition, anyone wanting to quit could; those who opted to stay either reenlisted or were re-commissioned in the Army of the United States. (AUS). Twenty-five percent of the enlisted women bowed out as compared to only a small fraction of the officers. Until this imbalance finally corrected itself, Officer Candidate School (OCS) was closed to all comers. Because the WAC only accepted for OCS those with prior enlisted service, the entire recruitment effort at that time was aimed at refueling the ranks.

By late summer, the situation became sufficiently desperate: I was invited, in a "we have good news for you" letter, to join. As a Private. The subject of my weight, to which I had added not one ounce, never came up.

Ethel Allen Starbird enlisted in the Women's Army Corps on September 28, 1943.

Two

Learning the G.I. Jive

I SHAMBLED off to war on September 28, 1943 with a set of golf clubs I was told I'd have ample opportunity to use, a going-away watermelon from my mother, my dad's World War I ear plugs, and a rural recruit named Ames who had never stirred farther from her birthplace than the local Grange Hall.

Quick to sense my leadership qualities, the Recruiting Officer put me in charge of both of us for the two-day trip to Des Moines, appointing me a temporary Corporal, a rank I would not achieve again for almost two years. Mine would not be a meteoric rise in the military.

Ames immediately became home sick and wept quietly most of the way to Chicago; even when not in tears she was about as chatty as a Carmelite.

It soon became apparent that a watermelon is an awkward snack in a Pullman seat – so I sent mine forward to happify the dining-car crew. The golf clubs, instead of providing a little distraction from the drill field, were confiscated by a company clerk who shipped them back home at a cost to me of almost my entire month's salary, then $50. The ear plugs disappeared much later in the Philippines: I suspected the "house boy" who never indicated by word or deed he ever heard a word I said.

RUTLAND ARMED FORCES INDUCTION DISTRICT
OFFICE OF THE COMMANDING OFFICER
38½ CENTER STREET

SPECIAL ORDER   RUTLAND, VERMONT
NUMBER 133   28 September 1943
                        E X T R A C T

          *   *   *

    Par. 1. Pursuant to authority contained in ltr. HFSC, dated
20 Sept. 1943, SPKVK 300.4, the following named women, enlisted in
the Women's Army Corps, AUS, this date, will proceed without delay
from the Rutland Armed Forces Induction District, Rutland, Vermont
to the First WAC Trng. Ctr, Ft. Des Moines, Iowa for classes starting 30 September 1943, reporting to the CO upon arrival thereat for
Basic Training.

        AMES, Alice F. (Mrs.)   A-110162   St. Johnsbury, Vermont
     * STARBIRD, Ethel A. (Miss)   A-110163   Burlington, Vermont

 * Acting Corporal
X-ray of chest taken - result negative
All White

        Enlistees have not been vaccinated or inoculated at this
station. No clothing issued. WD AGO Forms #724, #28, #43 and copies
of orders normally included will be placed in the care of STARBIRD,
Ethel A. to be delivered to the CO, 1st WAC Trng. Ctr, Ft. Des Moines,
Iowa upon arrival thereat.

        The above enlistees left this station at 2:25 P. M. Last meal
furnished was the noon meal.

        The TC will furnish necessary transportation. I.G.F. in accord-
ance with AR 30-2215 the QMC will issue four (4) party meal tickets
for two (2) women for the journey. Unused tickets will be turned in
to the CO at duty station.

        TDN 1-5010 P431-02 A212/40425.

          *   *   *

                  By Order of Major ROBERTS:

                                              MATHIAS H. NEISS
                                              2d Lt., A. U. S.
                                              Adjutant
OFFICIAL

MATHIAS H. NEISS
2d Lt. A. U. S.
Adjutant

Starbird's enlistment orders to WAC Basic Training in Des Moines, Iowa.

Having been near-neighbor to Ft. Ethan Allen for more than a decade, the features of Des Moines held few surprises: both originated as Cavalry posts in the late 19th century, both lay close to the same latitude, both were built along similar lines from almost identical War Department blueprints then being followed all over the country.

Constructed largely of age-mellowed brick, and shaded by century-old elms, the main post looked rather like a small college campus – without the ivy. Officers' line and two-storied barracks with double-decked porches faced each other across a parade ground large enough for a cattle drive. To the east: non-commissioned quarters, administrative offices, various recreational and service facilities with warehousing and stables forming the outer rim.

The last horses in military service were mustered out of the Army in 1940; the first WACs mustered in two years later. Until the Corps could prepare its own members for command functions, a few veteran Cavalry officers and cadre, some still resplendent in boots, campaign hats, and swagger sticks, had been dragooned into training the new fillies.

First stop on the Basic odyssey: temporary lodging called "stable row," little changed since its original occupants except the removal of water buckets and feed bins. Here, in our first few days, we would learn the true meaning of togetherness. (Even our blankets read US.)

This became especially true in the partition-free lavatories where lidless commodes, spaced only inches apart, created an intimacy more conducive to constipation than contemplation. With our ages ranging from 20 to 50 years (the WAC's allowable limits) and shapes reflecting similar diversity, mob showering in multi-fauceted rooms about the size of a single horse stall certainly put us in touch with each other – the surface scrubbed was often not our own.

By the time of our arrival, the blockade on uniform procurement had lifted with everyone receiving from that granddaddy of one-stop shopping – the supply room – thirty-five items including comb, toothbrush, and one listed provocatively as "overshoes, low women's."

Created by Mainbocher, the WAVE uniform of basic blue emerged as stylish, coordinated, and becoming to everyone who wore it. The WAC uniform, put together by a mostly male committee, looked it. The color alone – discretely described by some as "Boston coffee," by others in much richer terms – was a real loser; whoever wore olive-drab to the senior prom?

Fabricated of the same depressing shade, the blouse (jacket) had for months defied corrective surgery from despairing supply-room seamstresses who snipped and tucked without achieving a proper fit. Shapely occupants, once buttoned in, could barely bend. The maker, as it developed, was still working from patterns proportioned for guy GIs. By the time I was outfitted, proper adjustments had been made; given my shape I doubt I'd have noticed the difference. Uncorrected for the duration were the shirt tails, little longer than a baby's bib, that fluttered free with each salute (except Hobby's; the Director had the smarts to piece extra material onto hers) and the frustrating four-in-hand, a devil's device named no doubt for the four hands required to tie it.

The necktie's two working ends, meant to be of matching length, were then tucked out of sight between the third and fourth shirt button. As a matter of practice, however, the two usually came cut inches apart, the short end too high to hide. A solution soon evolved: tie the darn thing once to perfection, use only the slip knot to get it on and off, and then never, ever re-tie it. The WAVES avoided the problem with a flat pre-tied bow which the post-war WAC belatedly adopted.

At a later date and different place, my 6'5" Army brother[2] asked me to buy him some ties on my next trip to the uniform store. No one told me they came in "his" and "hers" so I picked up a selection for us both in the WAC section. Dressed for duty in one, it reached only to his top shirt button.

As for the hat, it was never an overwhelming success. Hobby insisted on a distinctive design, one that would mark its wearers as members of the WAC and no other. In this she succeeded admirably. But many felt it only favored the one woman on whom all hats looked smashing – Hobby herself.

---

2   Starbird's brother, Alfred Dodd Starbird, served in North Africa and Europe during WWII, receiving three Distinguished Service Medals.

Shaped like a tuna tin with its lid pried back it was, admittedly, far less flattering than the roll brim WAVE model, another eventual WAC acquisition – but not until after its members suffered through several variations inspired more by Jeanette MacDonald than Charles de Gaulle. But as Hobby had loyalists point out, that early creation must have had some merit: limp look-alikes reappear regularly as authorized Army headgear; at present, they seem a permanent fixture.

To minimize the macho appearance of her troops here at home, Hobby disapproved of their wearing slacks on any but the grungiest jobs. As Iowa weather worsened and temperatures tumbled, the rest of us shivered in our six-gore skirts that fully exposed to updrafts the loin in winter – and just about everything else in that vicinity.

Considering what the Army wears today, I think we looked pretty natty. Now both genders, outfitted like storm troopers, clomp around in camouflaged romper suits and cement-crusher combat boots; even those with the most passive duties – cooks, clerks, hospital corpsmen – dress for an air drop on Anzio. Like Fred Astaire in a tank top. A Class A uniform, crisp, wrinkle-free, and once required for all off-reservation wear and most duties on it, is now seen about as often as the dress sword.

Once suitably coutured as the government saw it for whatever lay ahead, we moved from our former equine billet into a place called Boomtown, a fairly new expansion area of barracks located on an upgrade just south of the main post. It would house 120 of us for the next six weeks as Basic Company 14, 3rd Regiment.

At this point, hair was bobbed or rolled to just about the collar and personal jewelry reduced to a single inconspicuous ring or wedding set on the left hand (no dazzle permitted on the saluting one), a wristwatch, and a necklace of double dog tags. Since there was seldom a moment after lights-out when someone wasn't moving about, trying to sleep was like living in a temple full of wind chimes. Until the P.X. produced a chain with offset clips, those without cleavage enough for a sound-deadening slot could enlist someone at home to crochet a set of quieting covers. Lacking both cleavage and a mother adept at needlework, I continued to clank.

This was not my only problem in the chest area: my parents had insisted that I always wear another of their going-away gifts – a money holder designed to dangle inside my clothes while pinned for safety to my bra straps. (In a family of flat-fronted females, dad took a ribbing for having won a WWI citation for "exceptionally meritorious service at Brest.")[3]

With a figure about as voluptuous as a praying mantis, a bra was never an essential part of my wardrobe. I finally rigged the thing on a string around my neck, housing it inside my slip. With this arrangement it became impossible to fish for cash in public without drawing a crowd. Furthermore, if the bag contained more than a single bill I looked like a nursing Chihuahua.

Properly uniformed at last, we were whistled out into pre-dawn Des Moines to learn how to come to attention, salute, and master the rudiments of close order drill: 120 sleepwalking zombies wondering what the hell they were doing there.

Any compelling desire to look sharp at this ungodly hour was offset by an almost complete lack of interest – and, by a garrulous crow cawing cadence from a rooftop in exact imitation of the first sergeant, further confusing us with twice the normal number of beats.

Exaggerating unconsciously as we strove to perfect our military bearing, we fell in with shoulders unnaturally braced, arms jacked at the elbow, and – for no apparent reason – our bodies tipped forward from the ankles about 5 degrees off the perpendicular. At attention, we closely resembled corn stalks drying in a winter wind, a situation which took some serious non-com nagging to correct.

My particular posture drew immediate attention: in repose, it was said to resemble an overheated Hershey bar. The Army changed all that; I was soon sitting, standing, and sleeping (I suspect) as if skewered. To achieve this position, it became my practice to snap upright at the slightest provocation, vibrating like a tuning fork. Toward the end of my military career even Col.

---

3   Starbird's father, Brig. Gen. Alfred Andrews Starbird, received an Army Distinguished Service Medal for actions during World War I relating to "the planning, organization, and administration of the post and sub-posts of Brest, Base Section No. 5" in France.

Hobby commented on my eye-catching performance: "Can't you make her stop?" she asked rather plaintively of her assistant Pat Chance to whom I was detailed at the time. "All that twanging is getting on my nerves."

Saluting was not much of a challenge; we were soon pumping away like professionals. Some became so enchanted with the exercise they devised unnecessary ways to confront unwary, arm-weary officers and – in the gathering dusk – were even known to high-ball the lampposts.

Obviously the correct salute – rigid palm, stiff wrist, crisp arm chop to the brow – was not destined to stay that way long; senior WACs (who almost everyone else was) felt compelled to make a personal statement with an extra flourish or two. Some of the results were riveting; especially the casual, cupped hand gesture an outfielder might use to keep a fly ball out of his eyeball. Or the fling thing that ended like a Papal blessing. Once out on our own, most of us worked out our own variations.

Since placement rosters had not yet emerged from the orderly room, we were told to form up into squads in no particular order. One group who obviously had known each other in an earlier life fell in together and executed - with Rockette precision and without a single audible command – every marching maneuver in the drill manual. Coming to a halt before the platoon commander, they saluted smartly then stood at parade rest awaiting further orders. Lt. Millian, the object of their attention, seemed in a state of shock. Then she beamed, thinking no doubt that with recruits like these the next six weeks would be a romp. If so, she reckoned without the rest of us.

As it turned out, this select little group – which no one seemed to know anything about – had been WAAC reservists, most recruited the year before from among graduating college seniors by the Army Signal Corps and trained as WIRES – Women in Radio and Electrical Service – at Paul Smith College deep in the heart of New York's Adirondack Mountains. Bored by their remote surroundings, they had talked one of their enlisted instructors into teaching them close-order drill, even to the silent version. Upon the changeover to WAC status, they had been offered active duty or discharge (but not commissions as promised), some ending up splintered off into various Boomtown companies where they created a short-term sensation.

I, too, had early military training. The young boys in my neighborhood formed an army adept in the martial art of mud-ball warfare. They reluctantly allowed me to join (mainly because the ammunition was baked to rock hardness on my family's laundry stove) – but only as a nurse. Our dog and I soon wearied of trundling our ambulance – my snazzy red express wagon – in futile search for casualties after each skirmish, the fallen usually preferring their mother's ministrations to mine. Relief finally arrived in the person of a new little girl on the block that was immediately drafted as my replacement while I promoted myself to the warrior class, preparing for combat with broom stick, ashcan cover, and the rudiments of close-order drill, a rather loose interpretation of the Infantry concept. This included an about-face – a sort of "veronica" without the bull – that spun us in reverse, the direction we were usually going anyway. The closest I ever came to the correct technique included a modified pirouette, a little two-step shuffle, and a heel click that would delight the Kaiser – not exactly what the real Army had in mind.

Every time I tried to do it their way I swayed like a tree under axe attack, my feet coming to rest at right angles instead of the prescribed 45 degrees in what dance circles is referred to as Position 3. "Stunning," said Lt. Millian. "Balanchine? Bolshoi? The Ballets Russes? Sergeant, I think this one needs a little more work." To this day – and I admit the demand is not great – I cannot execute a fluid about-face and have my feet come out looking like anything but an unfortunate mistake.

In some ways Basic Training resembled summer camp – without bedtime milk and cookies. Among us were the same annoying few who greeted each dawn with mad little squeals of joy, attacking each chore like a merit badge candidate. Similar, too, were those forgettable moments of organized delight when some rosy-cheeked Lieutenant called us together for team sport and/or sing-alongs while others of her ilk, armed with clip-boards, lurked offstage evaluating our enthusiasm for doing things in groups.

The singing was the worst. High visibility on the playing field made it practically impossible to fake participation there. In the chorus, however, convincing lip-synching could be achieved without uttering a sound. Often our fearless leader was going it pretty much alone.

Programs usually featured such standards as "Duty" sung to the tune of the "Colonel Bogey March;" and endless rondeau called "Gee, Mom, I Want To Go Home", a hit of a hundred verses with no two people knowing the same ones; and – under duress – a rather maudlin piece of work known as "The WAC Hymn." During breaks in the concert-on-command, we usually belted out without urging that old British madrigal, "I Don't Want To Join The Army" – not on the approved list but a real mood-booster then and in the years to come.

Three

Straightening Up and Flying Right

S OMEWHERE EARLY on, we swapped blouse buttons and hat devices embossed with the WAAC buzzard, a sort of eagle with an attitude that looked somewhat like a melon-breasted booby, for the more benign bird – our national emblem – as worn by the AUS.

Saved from immediate extinction, however, was our lapel insignia bearing the likeness of Pallas Athena, an inspirational WAAC/WAC symbol who covered all the bases as the Greek goddess of war, wisdom, and virtue. My parents evidentially expected her influence to prevail: when I wrote mother some months later that I had gotten the Good Conduct Medal[4], her only comment was "I should hope so."

Buttoned in and stepping out, we marched. And marched. To classes, to meals, to parade formations, to nowhere in particular. Moving at the brisk clip the Army required involved stretching well beyond the popular conception of a ladylike stride – maybe not the full 30 inches expected of the men but certainly close to it. The result: an ungainly gait that made us look like we were plodding over plowed ground. Only Ames, whom I had conveyed

---

4   The Army Good Conduct Medal is awarded "for exemplary behavior, efficiency, and fidelity in active Federal Military service." In 1943 the criteria for this award was amended from requiring the completion of three years of active service to requiring the completion of one year of service while the United States is at war.

West, failed to notice; raised on a farm in northwestern Vermont, she had probably walked that way all her life.

For the short, stubby WACs, staying in step was no stroll in the park. Straining to keep pace with their long-limbed sisters activated the more generous parts of their anatomy, setting them swinging like metronomes in overdrive. At a distance, it was difficult to tell whether they had broken into double-time or were merely marching to a different drummer.

Physical demands might have slimmed down a few of our weightier members, had someone somewhere realized that women did not need the same rations as men – 3,000 calories a day. By the time this was reduced to 2,000 calories, many had acquired add-on poundage that would remain in place for years to come.

To further complicate the situation, no edible morsel of anything could remain on a turned-in tray, with the diner having limited influence over what got there in the first place. Faced, let us say, with a Mount Shasta of mashed potatoes, the server shoveled away pretty much ignoring who wanted what and how much. But even without forced feeding, there was a tendency to pack it in, especially among those recently arrived from the outside world of shortages and substitutes. Who wouldn't go a little berserk over butter after almost two years of the original oleo-margarine - achieved by manhandling a lump of vegetable fat with a small pellet of orange dye until the entire mass acquired the color and consistency of axle grease.

Raised in a household that always catered to my father's ulcer, leaving home cooking for mess hall fare represented very little sacrifice on my part. Mother's menus were nutritious enough, but about as tasty as tofu. By contrast, GI meals were generally seasoned, perhaps as much to disguise shortcomings in their preparation as to enhance their flavor. For whatever reason, they seemed a lot livelier than family menus where spaghetti sauce was nothing but unadorned stewed tomatoes, with salt and pepper not only absent from all recipes but taboo at the table as well. Commenting rather favorably on my change of diet in a letter home was a serious tactical error: never even *imply* that the Army cooks better than your mother. My cookie allowance suffered for the next two months.

Bedtime ranked right up there with mealtime as the best time of the day. Under the Army's rules of good housekeeping, our metal cot (in this case) must be made up with hospital precision, wrinkle-free and taut as a drum head. Their placement must alternate: head to wall, feet to wall all the way down the line. In this way late talkers could only chat with their neighbors' feet. To minimize reveille response time, an occupant slipped eel-like into the envelope of bed clothes, determined not to move again until 5:30 a.m. Driven to near-exhaustion during the day, this was not as difficult as it sounds.

Exiting with the same economy of motion, it was possible to tighten everything up again with a few sharp tugs from below, dusting under the bed as we did so. The extremely modest who insisted on dressing and undressing under the covers had a somewhat tougher time – especially those who emerged with their shoes and ties in place.

Once everyone was up and moving, the program picked up pace; early morning hours accommodated reveille formation, breakfast a half-mile down the road, the policing of individual areas as well as such shared space as latrines, hallways, stairs, and outside acreage.

To either tamp down food or tone up muscles, we engaged each weekday morning in calisthenics – a good bit of bouncing about more or less in unison. With so little poundage to haul about, I expected to excel at pushups; instead I either sagged to the floor or arced like a croquet wicket above it. Perhaps the exercise that inspired the greatest freedom of expression: a graceless maneuver called the squat thrust, a demanding display of bending, leaping and mule-like kicks somewhat suggestive of bullfrogs in heat.

An interesting sidebar to all this body building: while it was going on the menstrual cramps that had plagued me for years disappeared completely. Although, I doubt if a hitch in the Army is on the list of recommended PMS treatments.

After tidying up the premises, making a quick costume change to "A" uniforms, and taking a bracing hike to the main post, we sat through three hours of classes in such stimulating subjects as military courtesy, tables of organization, and hygiene, which, on good days, featured a loudly applauded training film. Not for its message, however: as soon as the house lights dimmed and the musical introduction faded, the audience slept – unnoticed and undisturbed until a Sousa march or something equally rousing signaled the end of the show.

Not all films invited slumber. For example, one made exclusively for the fellows, demonstrating in grim and graphic detail the causes and effects of venereal disease, played to an extremely alert and appreciative house. How it got into the WAC pipeline, hey, who cares?

Next to the audio-visuals (a term not then in general use), the most popular class was that of an understanding instructor named Longanecker who underscored various points in here lectures as "nice to know" and "need to know;" only when she so labeled the latter did anyone pay the slightest attention. But then, Basic was never noted for its scholarship.

Afternoons for the most part were devoted to more marching about, culminating in a retreat formation where we faced a blank wall and saluted a flag we never saw to a scratchy recording of the National Anthem, hardly an experience to stir patriotic fervor.

Having acquired three shots in the arm in a single trip to the dispensary (typhoid, tetanus, scarlet fever) some of us had the opportunity to consider the flag-lowering ceremony from an entirely different point of view.

We had been hot-footing it around the area all afternoon in an effort to discourage real or imaginary reactions to the load of antitoxins we had just taken aboard, a bit of psychology that seemed to work since we mustered at almost full strength when we assembled for retreat. But, with the wind blowing away from us, the distant genuine bugle notes which usually cued our cadre on when to start the proceedings could not be heard. So they guessed. Badly. We were left standing at attention, rigid as tent poles, for a full twenty minutes before anyone turned on the canned music. By that time, shot reactions had set in big time and only half the Company remained upright; the rest had either crumpled earthward or were being hauled back to barracks by their hardier comrades. Unfortunately, I was one of the fallen.

When I re-focused, Lt. Simander, an excellent but no-nonsense officer from another platoon, was leaning over me instructing two helpers in revival techniques. My blouse and tie were already off; shirt and skirt would soon follow. And so, too, would Lt. Simander's scathing comments about my undergarments.

"And they expect me to make a soldier out of someone who looks like **this**?"

She pointed with obvious disgust at my lingerie, white as swan feathers with only the merest touch of lace.

"Look at you – just look at you – you're still half civilian!"

"But, ma'm," I said, "didn't your mother make you wear clean underwear when you went out – just in case you were in an accident? Mine did. If I had on those tattletale Army khakis now, who'd know the difference?"

Simander suddenly recognized a more deserving case at the other end of the squad room.

With Basic winding down, the Company had shaped up sufficiently to participate in the weekly post-wide retreat held on the main parade ground. Here we heard an actual band (all WAC), witnessed the lowering of an actual flag, and participated in the precise choreography of several thousand actual women in what I had to admit was one helluva show – even to a dance finale performed by a company of black WACs sashaying back to barracks to an exuberant, swingy cadence not found in any Drill Manual.

Although that earlier Boomtown retreat had proved the downfall of many of us, it ranked as small beer compared to the massive fall-out we suffered from a mess-hall serving of tainted brussel sprouts (which I avoid at all times.) Consequently, I was spared a galloping case of food poisoning as were only eighteen others who also abstained. But a hundred or so of the less fortunate took to their cots suffering disruptive attacks on two fronts.

Care of the ailing fell to the able-bodied few, at a ratio of about six to one. After plumping pillows, distributing fire buckets to barf in, and filling canteens for hot water bottles, we survivors set about scrubbing the entire compound – barracks, day, orderly and supply rooms as well as outside areas – for Saturday inspection the next morning. The latrines were a real challenge; it's no simple task to blitz a bank of commodes almost continuously (and often vigorously) in use.

I had more than a passing interest in the clean-up: the

communal upset coincided with my election as acting company commander – a sort of queen for a day without perks or prizes. In fact, quite the opposite: I had to eat at the end of the chow line and sit up past bed check during my entire reign of two days.

This end-of-basic "honor" had nothing to do with my military proficiency, but everything to do with my next-cot neighbor named Schultz, a talented artist who had papered the barracks with cartoons and slogans in support of my candidacy and mine was the name most voters remembered at poll time, though I doubt if more than a handful knew to whom it belonged.

We, the work crew, had been granted special permission to labor as late as necessary to get the job done, which we did – until 3 a.m. the next day. We would have finished earlier if one of our dedicated number hadn't decided to swab a particularly grubby part of the wooden floor with undiluted Clorox. The result was about as inconspicuous as a searchlight in a bat cave. To tone down her effort to match the rest of the room, we roused a sickly Schultz from her bed of pain to mix a compatible pigment from cigarette ashes, outdoor dirt, stove cinders, shoe polish and – for that final touch – a dollop of chocolate frosting from someone's mother-made cake. Schultz admitted it was one of her greatest artistic triumphs.

When the inspection party arrived, the ailing – clad in pajamas as the authorized uniform of the day – rose to the occasion by teetering weakly to their feet. Having made this effort, they collapsed back into bed as we passed. When we doubled back toward the exit, those who didn't have their heads in the fire buckets were trying desperately to lie at attention. My place in all this pageantry: mutely bringing up the rear. Naturally we won the week's battalion banner; I rather suspect on spirit alone. I never had a command that pleased me more. (In fact, I never again had a command.)

Schultz and I were just recovering from our heady victory on the honorary C.O. campaign when we were summoned out of formation and sent off on an unnamed mission to an unmarked office in the main headquarters building. Schultz disappeared immediately behind closed doors while I tried to recall any misdemeanors I might have committed of late. When she reappeared, she beelined for the stairway without uttering a word, and it was my turn.

In a briefing whose purpose escapes me even to this day, an unidentified officer instructed me to write every Thursday without fail to a place called the Curtis Novelty Company at a Des Moines post office box, and report anything I observed of a "suspicious nature," a term as vague then as "sexual harassment" is today. I was cautioned in conspiratorial tones never, absolutely never, to discuss this assignment with anyone ever, repeat ever. But given the revelations of recent years, I doubt if doing so now will compromise national security. On leaving, I received 100 postage stamps and some cheap, unmarked stationary – receipt of which seemed to make me one of Smiley's people.

Everyday English was not acceptable spy-speak for these weekly bulletins; instead they must read like a toy salesman's report to his home office. I was given the code name of Blackshear; my mystery pen-pal at Curtis would be addressed as Blackwell. To demonstrate the quality and subtleties of our correspondence, here's an example: "Dear Blackwell: Your shipment of rubber ducks has been received and customer wildly enthusiastic. Everything doing well at this end. Best to the gang. Blackshear." Once I had perfected this particular message, I saw no reason to alter it for my entire career as an undercover agent.

Although Schultz and I spent our remaining Thursday nights like Buddhas on adjoining bunks carrying on our one-way correspondence with those friendly folks at Curtis, torture would not have forced us to share our secret – even with each other. Although it was obvious to both of us that we engaged in the same activity, we remained ever faithful to our trust until years later when Schultz began signing her occasional letters "Blackburn" below a sketch of a WAC, her face concealed by a pulled-down Hobby hat and turned up collar, sneaking into the Des Moines post office.

Before long I ran out of stamps, so I simply stopped sending non-messages to Curtis & Co. Whoever ran this cloak-and-dagger caper had more staying power than I; each time I skipped a week, or changed stations hoping to lost my identity along the way, some genie would loom up out of nowhere to remind me that Mission Control was taking the affiliation far more seriously than I.

Four

They've Got Me Where They Want Me

BY MID-NOVEMBER, we had zipped through the 5-week Basic course in slightly under 7 weeks (by Army reckoning, the first and last didn't count) and were awaiting with considerable impatience the posting of field assignments. Among the first to hear were those selected for WAC recruiting and training-center slots – sort of "in-house" duty almost nobody wanted. One of the few to avoid that fate or further schooling, Schultz galloped off to the Cavalry School at Ft. Riley, Kansas, to do something with the graphic arts and to strike a blow for fraternization by marrying her officer boss some 16 months later.

Although we believe patriotism had a great deal to do with our being where we were, it was not the only reason: our ranks were full with Rosies tired of riveting. Tillies fed up with office toil, teacher-types eager to quit the classroom. Most sought a complete change, a more challenging outlet for their energies, and a closer identity with the war effort. The Army had ideas of its own.

In those days there was none of this "be all you can be" business: what the Adjutant General, grand pasha of personnel, wanted, the Adjutant General (like Lola) got. If kitchens suffered from understaffing, he plucked reinforcements from the latest crop of Basics and sent them off to Cooks' and Bakers' School; if auto mechanics were in short supply, a stint at Motor Transport School could be his gift to the girl graduate, neither fascinating prospects for those thinking more Joan of Arc than corn beef hash or lube job.

However, those already proficient in one of the more "womanly" occupations of the day – clerk, typist, stenographer, teacher, telephone operator – would probably go right on doing much the same sort of job they had joined the WAC to escape. Among us, only the WIRES – whom we knew fondly as "wig-wag WACs" – already knew their military occupation, if not their destination. Pre-trained in communications, they would rejoin the Signal Corps as radio and cryptographic specialists.

Some of us with no trades or talents readily converted to military needs became candidates for Army clerkdom, shipping off to an Administration School to learn how it was done – in ten or more copies. That was the closest match the Army could manage to my former specialty[5] – writing advertising copy for such clients as Bag Balm and Kow Kare, two udderly soothing salves for the bovine set. Only one other member of our company had better credentials for military service; she had been as snake charmer in civilian life.

My destination, and that of some 130 other Boomtown basics, was Eastern Kentucky State Teachers' College in Richmond, Kentucky (pop: 7,300). There we would master the mysteries of such mind-expanding subjects as Morning Reports, Duty Rosters, and a real brain-number called Telegs, Radiogs, Cablegs, Mag Forms, and Melvile Dewey's wondrous Decimal Filing System which, to my knowledge, only the Library of Congress understands.

Getting there was not half the fun…

Since we lived then in a world more traveled by train than plane, every piece of rolling stock, regardless of age or rail-worthiness, had been recalled to active duty. Our three Pullman cars were perhaps the weariest of the lot. The sooty plush upholstery smelled of a million miles of coal dust, the lights remained in perpetual dim-out, the water cooler crawled with minute wild life, and we expected at any moment to be boarded by the James boys.

---

5   From 1941-43, Starbird worked at the Townsend Advertising Service in Burlington, Vermont.

Snorting steam and spewing cinders, an ancient coal burner towed us south.

Coupled to a wandering freight, we stuttered along for some 700 miles and 36 hours without food and with only one brief breath of fresh air – in Evansville, Indiana. Sleeping aboard for two nights produced the only spirited competition for upper bunks I have ever witnessed: due to space limitations, double occupancy was required for the more accessible berths below – and no one wanted to lose what little privacy sleep-time allowed. And divvying up that little fish-net hammock strung across the lower window was a real problem – it would barely hold one pair of WAC field shoes, let alone two.

In those days, rail travel, erratic at best, guaranteed two absolute certainties: all scenic wonders would pass unseen in the middle of the night, and destinations – regardless of scheduled arrival times – would be reached between 3 and 5:30 in the morning. Richmond was no exception.

Eastern Kentucky State Teachers' College, now simply Eastern Kentucky University, then consisted almost entirely of a quadrangle of pseudo-Colonial buildings fringing the natural amphitheater of a bowl-shaped ravine. By the time we debarked, 3:30 a.m. the campus was already showing signs of neglect. Small wonder. Opened in 1942, the number of paying students had since dwindled to one-fifth normal enrollment; the use of its facilities by a unit of the Army Specialist Training Program (ASTP) and a contingent of WACs probably kept its doors open through 1943 and 1944.

Having the ASTP men around after the dating drought of Des Moines did nothing to improve our social life: mixing occurred only at mealtime and then only at separate tables. But, of course, they were officer material, we were not. Which may be why they all appeared one morning – whether from boredom or rebellion we don't know – with their crew cuts dyed a screaming chrysanthemum yellow.

Considered in its entirety, the place suited our purposes well. Our billet, called Burnham Hall, housed, besides us, such amenities as a post office, vest-pocket Post Exchange (PX), laundry service, orderly room, dispensary, and one slightly warped ping-pong table. The dining hall, a rather elaborate affair dripping with chandeliers and voluntarily staffed with a flock of jolly local ladies who believed no one was properly served without a dollop of lumpy hominy, was practically next door; our class rooms only a block away. Here we would spend close to another seven weeks (this time first and last <u>did</u> count) learning to turn out the quantity and quality of paperwork the Army so much admires.

As for my role, it would continue but under slightly different ground rules as I discovered when an envelope appeared beneath my door marked, with questionable restraint, <u>PRIVATE, CONFIDENTIAL, EYES ONLY.</u> It summoned me to a cadre room at the far end of the basement for a clandestine rendezvous with a WAC sergeant who bore a remarkable resemblance to Victor McLaughlin. Making sure no one else was in sight; she yanked me into her quarters and pulled down all the shades. The tattoo on her forearm did nothing to reassure me.

About the time I got ready to bolt, she moved closer, blocking the door. "We know all about you Blackshear," she hissed – an unsettling declaration under the best of circumstances, which these were definitely not. "Your responsibilities will go on as before. But I will handle your weekly reports. Double seal each one in two envelopes placing them under my door when you're absolutely sure the corridor is totally empty and no one sees you."

As if I'd venture that way under any other conditions.

"What if I have nothing to report?" I asked.

"Report it anyway."

Which, for my stay in Kentucky I did – reporting dutifully that I had nothing to report. Fortunately none of my classmates asked what I was doing spooking around in the nether regions which, as cadre country, none of us visited from choice.

For the most part, our time was spent in the classroom perfecting our typing and filing skills which many of us knew already. But what we hadn't known before was the Army wrote in a language all its own – a kind of cryptography that dispensed with most vowels and an occasional consonant to produce such gibberish as "rptng co for dy GHQ, tral MCC, mon alws in lieu of rat and qtrs atzd." – a gibberish from which today's classified ads and cyberspeak obviously descend. With practice, the result became decipherable but impossible to articulate – except perhaps by a Slovak-Cambodian.

The Army also did some weird things with the spoken work like insisting "oblique" rhyme with "ike" and "route" with "out," supposedly to avoid such slushy syllables as "eek" and "oot" which carry poorly as field commands.

Very little in the way of entertainment interrupted our studies. Unless you count a Saturday afternoon visit to a horse farm to admire from afar the aging and already-pasturized Man O'War, a retired race horse of considerable distinction, and discovering in the process that blue grass wasn't blue at all.

On one other occasion, we trooped off to a tobacco warehouse where the auctioneer's chant echoed through the hanger-like structure as clearly and precisely as that of early airport announcers, who must have learned diction at the same place doctors learned penmanship.

At rare moments we did engage in one other off-duty activity worthy of mention: the clandestine consumption of some of the worst corn whiskey in all Kentucky, bootlegged at $20 a pint through the back door of a local pool hall. The fiery contraband was later dispensed in microscopic portions to paid-up members of our limited partnership as we skulked in concealing shadows of the football bleachers.

Transferring from dry Des Moines to a part of the country deservedly famous for its hospitality and juleps, we naturally expected a warm welcome and at least the availability of a beer, a mainstay in PXs elsewhere but not in ours. However, one of our number named Blanton, kin to half the county, blew our hopes; she explained that the locals voted the town dry as soon as they heard the WACs were on the way.

Luckily Lexington, a tweedy sort of place 30 miles up the pike, had a friendlier attitude. A week or so before Christmas we were each given a $25 partial payment out of a private's monthly total of $50, and an overnight pass – our first since enlisting – to explore its delights. Which we almost didn't…

To explain: the Army, in its generosity, had issued each of us a heavy winter overcoat and a lighter "utility" coat for warmer and rainier weather. When the uniform of the day called for one, the other hung in the closet buttoned over a regulation shoulder purse hooked out of sight on the same hanger. Since no place on our persons could carry anything that wouldn't create a forbidden bulge, the purses served instead, holding all the usual: cosmetics, photos, wallets, cigarettes, stuff.

The Tuesday before our scheduled bug-out to Lexington, some light-fingered felon cruised the dorm while we were in class, undoing middle coat buttons, rifling purses, cleaning us out to our last dollar (only loose change was spared.) Once word was out and losses confirmed, we were ordered to remain at attention downstairs while the officers and cadre searched us for non-anatomical contours some $3,000 in small bills would create. Coming up empty, they then fanned out through the building for what was euphemistically called a "shakedown inspection." Again no illegal loot was found – not even the pricey pint of Christmas cheer resting on the bottom of our toilet tank.

Why so much time was wasted on our student bodies remains a mystery since only cadre and college staff had access to the building when the heist took place. Only someone extremely familiar with our regimen would know where to look and when – which seemed to narrow the field of suspects to those actually in the billet at crime time. No culprit was ever found. But someone – bless him/her – found $3,000 in government funds to reimburse us for our losses – and Lexington survived our *anschluss* without too much trauma.

As a prelude to graduation, my musically minded roommate, Marian Walsh, and I were volunteered by someone of higher authority who wisely remained anonymous to write the score and book for the class's final show. Inspired by the patriotic extravaganzas of the moment, we assembled a DeMille-sized cast, most for a chorus only slightly smaller than the Mormon Tabernacle Choir that belted out Walsh originals whenever the action lagged – which was frequently. In our over-zealous casting we had, however, all but eliminated the audience, leaving no one to watch but the faculty and custodial help. Even after opening the doors to the ASTP, the genuine college kids, and anyone who happened by, we still played to a thin, albeit responsive, house.

The program ended on a high note – full chorus at full volume singing the Walsh finale:

"Now that the time is nigh to say goodbye
Mixed in with all our cheer you'll hear a sigh.
For we want you to know as you see us go
Part of our heart will remain
With the things that we all must have gained
From just knowing you…"

Not exactly Cole Porter – but given our impending departure we could almost believe Walsh's soupy sentiments. By then, assignment fever completely absorbed us; we talked and thought of little else. Having spent more than three months honing our skills for some place vaguely referred to as "the field" – which, loosely translated, meant anywhere we weren't – we felt way past ready for a regular job.

WOMEN'S ARMY CORPS BRANCH NO. SIX
ARMY ADMINISTRATION SCHOOLS
RICHMOND, KENTUCKY

TO ALL WHOM IT MAY CONCERN:

This is to Certify That

ETHEL A. STARBIRD   A-110163

has diligently pursued and successfully completed the course of instruction in Basic Administration at WAC Branch No. 6, Army Administration Schools, 20 November 1943 to 12 January 1944. Appropriate notation of such accomplishment has been entered on her record.

The completion of this course of study indicates that this enlisted woman of the WAC is qualified to perform the duties of Public Relations Man having graduated with an average grade of 94; typing 56 WPM; and taking dictation at the rate of _____ WPM.

The course of instruction at this school consisted of the following:

Subjects:	Hours:	Subjects:	Hours:
Absences of Personnel	6	Morning Reports	12
Administrative Exercises	12	Non-Military Correspondence	3
Administrative Problems	20	Officers Status Cards	1
Allotments	3	Orders and Publications	12
Authorized Abbreviations	1	Organization of Post, Camp, & Sta. Hq.	4
Chain of Command & Channels of Communication	1	Organization of the Army	5
Classification & Assignment	5	Pay & Allow of EM & O incl. WAC	14
Courtesies & Customs of the Service	1	Per Diem, Mileage, Baggage, & Depend. Alws.	2
Courts-Martial Administrative Procedure	4	Postal Service	2
Current Changes in AR's & Current Events	7	Property Procurement and Accounting	16
Discharges & Releases	2	Psychology of the Soldier	2
Duties & Responsibilities of NCO	1	Safeguarding Military Information	3
Duty Roster	2	Service Record	12
Filing	10	Sick Report	2
Insurance	2	Soldiers & Sailors Civil Relief Act	1
Investigations & Board of Officers	4	Study Habits and Procedure	1
Machine Records Procedures	7	Telgs, Radiogs, Cablegs, Msg. Form	3
Maint. & Use of AR's, WAC Reg. & Other Mil. Publ	4	Transfers	1
Military Correspondence	19	Typewriting	35
Mimeographing	2		

Louis W. Eggers

LOUIS W. EGGERS
Lieutenant Colonel, Infantry
Commanding

Upon completion of Army Administration School, Starbird was qualified to serve as a "Public Relations Man."

Five

Moonlight in Boston

A SIZEABLE share of the class would end up in the Army Transportation Corps, prime mover of men and material which involved, among other responsibilities, operating the nation's overworked ports of embarkation. Since all of those were located in or near key coastal cities, those of us selected for this particular branch of service could reasonably expect to participate once again in at least the fringe benefits of civilization.

Of particular promise within this context: Boston where some fifteen of us would form the nucleus for the first-ever WAC detachment stationed at its port of embarkation.

In this Athens of the Americas, culture – as its citizens tirelessly pointed out – was as much a staple of daily life as baked beans and scrod on the breakfast menu. We had missed little during our exile. For, here in the home of Fiedler and Koussevitzky, the hills (Beacon, Copp's, Blue, etc.) were alive with the sounds of such major musical works as "Mairzy Doats," "The Hut-Sut Song," and "Cement Mixer (Puti Puti)."

So much for exposure to the arts.

As it turned out, we had little time to sample the best of Boston, preferring when free time permitted to explore the classical attractions of Schollay Square rather than those of the Atheneum or Gardiner Museum.

Upon arrival at the BPOE (aka the Boston Army Base) we were supposedly posted to jobs that might achieve a major WAC objective: to release a GI for combat. Except me. I reported to the Message Center where I released a GS-2 civilian for an uninterrupted, day-long coffee break. That recruiting message about freeing a fellow to fight did not endear us to those we had come to replace, or their kin-folk. And it sure put a damper on our social life: "Dating a WAC under these conditions," wailed one arm-chair commando, "would be like dating your draft board."

So much for love among the manifests.

While some WACs then filtering into Boston drew quarters in private downtown clubs relinquished for the duration, we took up residence at the Franklin Square House, 11 East Newton Street, a rather gloomy old pile in a downscale neighborhood, tenanted at the time primarily by women, many well past retirement age.

As a matter of policy when the Army requisitioned living space off-base, it tried to avoid a mix of military and civilian personnel – but some of the Franklin Square ladies were far too entrenched to dislodge. Besides, we were too few in the beginning to require much space, so we occupied double rooms at one end of an upper floor cleared for our arrival. Ours was an elongated and often lonely stretch of property where we could have bowled in the hallway without disturbing anyone but ourselves – except possibly the cadet nurses from Boston City Hospital living one flight below.

Mothers, worried that their daughters turned loose in the city would become improper Bostonians, had absolutely nothing to fear: the front door was bolted promptly at 10:00 p.m.; the only way in after that meant waking up an ogre of a night clerk to face her unfailing wrath. Besides, the most inviting parts of Schollay Square were already off-limits, depriving us of the midnight show at the Old Howard, the spinning tassels of Sally Keith at the nearby Crawford House, and the escorts who wanted to take us there.

So mostly we stayed home. Indoor recreation also left something to be desired. Smuggling forbidden distillates in and empties out disguised as dirty laundry was about as exciting as things got. Only the elevator boy, age 81, correctly identified the clink in our barracks' bags, selling his silence for $5 a week, which he called a tip rather than the blackmail it really was.

On the whole, life in Boston was not too different from the civilian one we'd left behind. Like real-life folks, we commuted to work by bus, were spared physical therapy (PT), kitchen patrol (KP) and drill. Gone a glimmering was the 44-hour work week and its useful byproduct, overtime pay. We regularly put in 50 to 60 hours on the job, and then spent free nights on the docks volunteering to check boarding rosters and to exchange small talk with the outbound, just hoping it would help.

Although assigned to a double room, I enjoyed the luxury of a single since Olive Slattery, who was meant to share it, had family in nearby Farmingham where she spent most nights and weekends. Lieuts. Colvin and Dickerson, in charge of the Port's WAC contingent, lacked my luck.

Billeted as roommates at the end of the hallway, they could not escape 24-hour duty or a near-steady stream of callers. To discourage long visits from those of us determined to help them run the company properly, they simply removed all chairs from their room – forcing me to campaign for a new assignment from their wastebasket. I bore the imprint of this engagement for weeks.

While other military careers skyrocketed, mine began at the bottom and just sort of stayed there. Whereas time in grade between Private and PFC was then about three months, I'd already remained stripeless for six, with no one clamoring to change things. It had become evident that the only way to greater glory lay in lateral moves like the one then under negotiation with Colvin and Dickerson.

As it turned out, both of them were already lobbying for broader job opportunities for WACs, feeling any increase would make enlistment more attractive. (The Corps would soon coddle new recruits with their choice of job and station.) Personally, I think it was only a desire to empty their wastebasket that led to my transfer to the Port's all-male public relations staff, most of local origin modeled more after Marquand's George Apley than Mauldin's Joe and Willie.

For me, "public relations" proved a rather loose term. For

starters, I was detailed to the Publications Branch to illustrate a training manual on the care and operation of fork lifts, which my Mitty side only wanted to drive. Instead, equipped with a sort of thumb-screw device called a Leroy Pen, I managed to convert perfectly understandable photographs into line drawings with no artistic ability whatsoever.

Then, on an unseasonably hot day in May, I was sent off to the Boston Marathon to drive a WAC-laden amphibious DUKW[6] shaped like an undernourished coal barge down 26-plus miles of race route. The purpose of this exercise: to demonstrate the fun, fellowship, and high adventure awaiting those who join the Corps. Incinerated by sun baked steel and winter uniforms as we awaited our turn at the top of Commonwealth Avenue, I doubt that we tempted anyone.

Having noticed our extreme discomfort, a kindly gentleman handed up two fistfuls of ice cream cones from a vendor's cart in the hope of cooling us down. As we lapped happily down the first long hill, I thought I was doing rather well, never having been in a DUKW before, to navigate one through a totally unpredictable sea of spectators. That is, until a churlish Colonel, dripping with ribbons and indignation, stopped me with a bellow probably heard in Provincetown:

*"**Get rid of that food! Now!** And be quick about it!"*

Slattery was the first to recover from the attack: "Where, sir?"

"Dammit, I don't care where. Anywhere! Anyhow! Just do it – and fast!"

If any litter laws existed in those days, no one took them seriously. So, bewildered but obedient, we jettisoned the cones onto the street below. The Colonel had more to say on the subject. "Don't you women know anything? You're soldiers now. You should have learned that no one in Army uniform, regardless of rank, ever – repeat ever – appears in public eating, carrying parcels or an umbrella or…" since we were all standing at attention anyway, he checked our waistlines "…or pushing a baby carriage." (Poor man, he probably never lived to see pregnancy uniforms.)

Assuming our presence at the Marathon was aimed at attracting

---

6   A DUKW, commonly called a "duck," is a six-wheel-drive amphibious truck that was designed by General Motors for use during World War II.

attention (and not to distract Clarence DeMar who, as I did, spent student time at the University of Vermont[7]) we had succeeded beyond all expectations. Thanks to the Colonel who was getting a healthy Fenway Park boo as we motored out of earshot.

Again calling it public relations so I couldn't rebel, Dickerson sent me off one Sunday afternoon to Cambridge for four o'clock tea with two elderly sisters who "wanted to do their part for the war effort." The pen of Mary Petty might have created both their Chauncey Street residence and its occupants; greeting me clothed, coiffed, and perfumed in various intensities of lavender, they led me into a library of genteel shabbiness, books stacked to the ceiling with even one of those rolling ladders to reach them, leather chairs that made rude noises when sat upon, and everywhere family photos of Barnstable summers and student days at Harvard.

My hostesses and I swapped Military trivia, theirs deriving largely from memories of the earlier Roosevelt – "the good one" – and Dewey's derring-do at Manila Bay. The maid, Edwardian in age and apparel, made passing the see-through bread-and-butter sandwiches seem like an act of personal sacrifice, which it may well have been given wartime shortages and rationing restraints. In this household, however, status – as rated by these Cambridgians – seemed to determine the menu. For, as I was leaving, the next guests arrived for high tea as compared to my low one. The maid reappeared, this time trundling a cart generously laden with jelly tarts, fruit cake slices, cinnamon toast, and scones.

The Chauncy Street sisters, whose ancestors probably balked at breaking bread with the Indians that first Thanksgiving, could have learned a lesson in hospitality from the Captain of a Norwegian freighter idled in Boston harbor for the duration because his ship lacked the horsepower to keep up with convoys headed eastward. When he requested the pleasure of our company for Sunday smorgasbord and a ship's tour, he really meant our company – all of it. Eager for a change from scrod, we accepted enthusiastically and en masse.

Once aboard and after a brief demonstration of cargo handling

---

7   Starbird graduated from the University of Vermont in 1938 with a degree in Economics.

(with several references to what sounded to me suspiciously like "Starbird wench") he and his crew laid out a spread featuring every Scandinavian delicacy that ever swam, mooed, cackled, or oinked. Which left their cupboard completely bare of their favorite foods, available if at all only on the other side of the Atlantic. Yet when Slattery praised the kippers, the skipper wanted to send her home with those still on the plate.

Game, set, and match to Norway.

When I was not out relating to the public – in the broadest possible terms – I concentrated on promoting the crusade of Commanding General C. H. Kells to discourage public discussion of port activities. Although 19th century expansion had mowed down many of Boston's original hills from which early settlers – a seafaring lot – commanded an unobstructed view of maritime traffic, 20th century residents could survey much the same scene from many a multi-storied building in the city.

Further, from certain unrestricted sites, it was possible – with a pair of field glasses – to count and identify almost everything being loaded aboard outbound ships. The General's concern was fully justified.

Unable to completely camouflage port activities, Kells decided to emphasize the dangers of talking about them with a slogan blitz aimed at the general population "a slip of the lip can sink a ship," "loose talk loses lives," "zip your lip – save a ship," "keep mum, chum." With these and similar sentiments, we papered the city – from bar coasters to 24-sheet billboards, from washroom mirrors to public telephone booths, from transit tickets to restaurant table tent cards. Pedestrians bent over at their own risk. About the only space we missed were the headboards on the beds at the Parker House.

The legwork involved in plugging this message was mostly mine, taking me into the executive offices of Mayor Maurice Tobin, the brewery of Mr. Heffenreffer, the betting booths of the Wonderland Race Track, and the dressing room of Gracie Fields then playing at a downtown club, and – most happily – just about every tavern in town.

Believing that they had at last slotted me into the right job – and that their most persistent complainer was out of their hair and their wastebasket – the Lieutenants were about to retrieve their chairs when I reappeared on their threshold: "Don't you think, ma'ms, that it's about time I went overseas?"

"Hold the chairs," cautioned Colvin.

"Fact is, Private," said Dickerson, "that thought never occurred to me. You certainly haven't exhausted all the possibilities we have to offer. Let's see, how long have you been here anyway?"

"Going on three months," I said.

"Barely going *off* two," Colvin amended.

"But, gee, Lieutenants ma'ms, couldn't you consider it favorably now that I've brought the matter up?"

"Probably not," said Dickerson. "As I recall you came into the Army with a 274 MOS, public relations specialist, right? Not very useful at the time so off you went to Ad School to become a proficient clerk-typist – MOS 247. Which you were when we acquired you. Then we had you reclassified back to a 274, pretty much at your insistence as I recall, so you'd qualify for a PR job. But, the only MOS anyone seems to want overseas except infantry man is – guess what – a 247."

"I'll take it!"

"Get that in writing," advised Colvin.

On entering service, every WAC received a "Military Occupation Specialty number" (MOS) which, in many cases, was the code designation of the type of work she had never done in civilian life but for which the Army felt her admirably suited once she became the girl with the star-spangled heart. (Thus a WAC I knew named St. Peter became a natural for a job as a Chaplain's Assistant.)

When a Theater command needed non-combat help, a request went out to the War Department where it was assigned the appropriate MOS then circulated to the field for action. Those with required skills – if they wanted to go – were eligible for selection. The only other consideration: to be liked – or disliked – enough to be released. Whatever motivated the Lieutenants in my case, I never asked.

However, before the month ran out, Dickerson had re-juggled my numbers yet again, putting me almost back where I started – to a 247. And I was on my way out of the country with a slight detour to Ft. Oglethorpe, Georgia, to learn how to behave when I got there. Of some 400 from all over with similar orders, I may well have been the only one who knew exactly where we were going.

Although this information was highly classified, as were all troop movements, every port knew the destination of every shipment going anywhere. Working in troop control, my roommate Olive obviously knew where everyone was headed, including me.

Returning from work a few days later, I found her sitting on the floor, a map of the world spread out before her; we kept it on hand to track the war's progress. Since my outbound orders had been cut, it was a safe bet she knew where my shipment – RW999C – was going. But this being top secret information, she was duty bound not to tell. And, naturally, I felt duty bound to find out.

"Aw, c'mon, Olive," I wheeled, "you know I'll never tell."

"Neither," she declared indignantly, "will I."

"At least give me a clue. Which continent?"

"No way. My lips are zipped."

"Okay! Okay! How about which hemisphere?"

"Torture will not make me tell."

"Certainly you can say whether it's above or below the Equator."

"I'll go to my grave first."

Happily, she didn't have to resort to any such extreme. But true to her trust, she never uttered a single hint. Instead, while I was taking my shower, she put a spare blouse button on Brisbane, Australia, and went off to supper humming "Waltzing Matilda."

I was delighted. This would be new territory for WACs which I would probably never see except by going overseas as a guest of a grateful nation. I certainly never expected to get there by going abroad. There is a difference of course: abroad means you pay for it; overseas means someone else does.

While in Boston, my correspondence with Curtis ceased completely - never to be resumed; not one report on the condition of the local rubber-duck market. But evidentially a more diligent mole operated among us; I'd barely left South Station before a dour German-born member of our detachment was summarily detached for duration duty in deepest Montana. Whatever the cause, I couldn't quite see her signaling U-boats from the roof of the Franklin Square House (which cabbies preferred to call Franklin's warehouse.) But then, back in 1775, the British might have fared better had they suspected someone was hanging a lantern aloft in the Old North Church.

Being forewarned about our Brisbane destination when I got to Oglethorpe launched me into a brief but rewarding criminal career – as an insider trader. With revealing where we were going, I wagered three month's pay among my fellow travelers on where we weren't: England or North Africa, the only two areas overseas known at that time to be open to WACs. (Unknown to us, the first WAC contingent had already sailed for Australia, news that could have seriously undercut my odds making.)

Six

Deep in the Heart of Georgia

Practically everyone reaching Oglethorpe in those days, whether from Presque Isle, the Presidio, or WAC-stops in between, arrived aboard the Chattanooga Choo Choo which dropped post-bound passengers in its namesake Tennessee city just above the Georgia border. Here we were met, as the song goes, by a "certain party at the station" (a sergeant definitely not called "funny face"), piled into 6-by trucks, and relayed with considerable abandon the last 11 miles.

Not surprisingly, considering their horse Cavalry origins, Oglethorpe bore a strong family resemblance to Forts Ethan Allen and Des Moines, but had been greatly expanded from its original layout to accommodate its role and recruits as the Third WAC Training Center. The reservation itself, not a particularly impressive piece of real estate, sprawled southward from just below the Tennessee line to the Civil War battlefield of Chickamauga which buffered the south and southeast portions of the post. (That part known as South Post, added for wartime purposes, long ago reverted to the National Park from which it was whittled.)

One particular venue – the Extended Field Service Battalion – lay in the far northeast corner nudging a sweep of red dirt, scrub, and scrawny pines which, as scenery goes, left a great deal to be desired. What lay in the west, none of us knew or, quite frankly cared.

So situated, we were obviously outside the improvement perimeter for our home while becoming overseas-oriented was an abandoned, weather-beaten old Civilian Conservation Corps camp close by an equally isolated but fully occupied German POW stockade, both well over a mile from the main post and its amenities. The only apparent conversion made to accommodate female tenants: a quick sex-change of the latrines which left them looking much like those on Des Moines'"stable row." As a further indignity: our white bath towels were taken away for fear, no doubt, a future washday display in some far land would invite enemy attack. Khaki substitutes, temporarily stuck in a supply pipeline, appeared weeks later; in the meantime, air-drying so many bodies was a truly awesome sight.

The extremes of north Georgia climate made from some lively choreography in the shower and some strange bedfellows in the barracks. Stressed by widely fluctuating temperatures, the floor boards, laid on stringers close to the ground, had separated, providing easy access above for critters nesting below, the insect population having earned the place the soubriquet "bedbug row." Being unfamiliar with the local fauna and not really caring to learn, we simply rolled papoose-fashion into our blankets, yielding the floor to the squeakers of the house.

Most of us had come in from the field outfitted in uniforms painstakingly matched and remodeled over a period of months to form-fitting perfection. Almost immediately these along with every other item charged to our clothing and equipment allowance was put to the test to determine its fitness for foreign service. To make a proper evaluation, two rather substantial non-coms tugged, twisted, stomped, and mangled each piece so lovingly assembled and, when all else failed, grabbed a corner and ran off in opposite directions. The slightest flaw meant rejection; when the trials were over, I had been reduced to little more than a comb and toothbrush.

At a warehouse the next day I picked up my replacements for what I had come to regard as a very tidy and serviceable wardrobe. Added to my former issue at that time: four Hobby hats (decidedly a case of overkill), 2 sets of fatigues, and one extra pair of field boots (which I retain in hopes of having them cast in bronze one day.) Oh, yes, and 1 pair of 4-buckle Artics (not to be confused with overshoes, low women's). As impressive and ill-fitting as all this new finery was, we were forbidden to wear or alter any of it – it was our going-away outfit.

Instead, we spent all day every day in the same shredded, drop-seat coveralls that had clothed earlier overseas trainees during the past six months. Based on two-week turnovers, that's an amazing amount of wear and tear. Instead of one size fits all, no size fit anyone. Consisting of a yard or so of light-weight twill held together with safety pins, adhesive tape, and sheer perseverance, they were worn through the gas chamber, over muddy Georgia roads, on KP and sometimes, when we were too tired to change, to bed. The greatest insult of all was paying a 25¢ deposit to borrow what surely were the most fatigued fatigues – the most distressed dress – in the entire U.S. Army. Sew a designer label in them today and they'd outsell Calvin Klein.

Being authorized only one set of these little beauties in a southland spring that seldom stopped dripping, washing and drying them between formations became an impossibility; crud clung to them tighter than barnacles to a whale's tail.

It made no difference if those within stood at starch-stiff attention, those coveralls remained forever at ease. On the move, we resembled a rummage sale waiting to happen.

Lacking long underwear to insulate us from the still-nippy weather, we took to wearing our flannel pajamas not only at night but through the mounting temperatures of the daylight hours as well. Their comfort in the morning became a torture by noon. As the sun rose higher and sweat poured more freely from our pores, the pajamas shrunk to tourniquet tightness around upper arms and thighs where they had been shoved to escape detection. Relief must wait until after duty hours by which time the dew or heavier was falling, making it impossible to try anything. Slithering shower-soaked bodies into damp nightclothes was about as easy as getting into a rubber bathing suit (whose fashion life was thankfully short.) So the cycle began anew each morning as our leaders arrived to amuse us.

The first few hours were pretty much Basic redux: reveille formation, breakfast, barracks' clean-up (somewhat simplified by floor cracks), a little muscle toning, then off to classes to learn the perils of phosgene, marvels of the modern slit trench with a do-it-yourself demonstration on how to build one. Also on the agenda: first aid, chemical warfare, malaria control, military customs and courtesy, wear and care of the uniform, map reading, and a refresher course in sex from which the only new thing we learned as that one of those in the class was the mother of the Lieutenant giving it.

There were, of course, other forms of busy work. Without fail, in fair weather and foul, we walked. Calling it marching would mislead: after the first fifteen minutes on the trail, military bearing dissolved, we scuffed through field and forest at no particular cadence looking about as soldierly as Union troops retreating from Chickamauga back in 1863.

The first few days involved nothing more strenuous than short bird walks in Chickamauga Park, poking along admiring its monuments and natural attractions as the smoky woods of winter evolved into the gentle greens of spring. By the second week, these leisurely strolls had stretched into ten- and twelve-mile hikes – still no major problem as long as we transported only ourselves.

Which lasted until the posted order-of-the-day read: "turn out at 0700 in full field equipment including canteen, First Aid kit, helmet, and 30-pound pack." Actually, that was far from "full field equipment" since we also had been issued gas mask, mosquito bar, head net, 3 bottles of insect repellant, leggings, pistol belt, mess kid, sun glasses, shoulder harness and – perhaps to suggest that we really were headed for Old Blighty – that pair of four-buckle Artics.

But the lesser load was quite enough.

My first effort to assume a combat ready appearance failed to inspire. To meet the 30-pound minimum, I stuffed my pack (actually called a musette bag) with bricks from a nearby cellar hole and both pairs of field boots, creating so many sharp edges my back complained for days. Then, too, the milk I had so cleverly chosen over water to fill my canteen quickly churned itself into a solid leaving me parched for the entire day. Fortunately, no emergency required use of the First Aid kit, the contents of which I regard with the same ignorance and unease as those of a sewing kit.

At the end of five miles, we peeled off our gear preparatory to a "take ten" break. Bedded in the cool grass, sucking on a Lucky Strike (then the cigarette of choice) we barely noticed the arrival of a jeep bearing a picture-perfect Special Services officer, and my God - balls, bats, and gloves! To keep morale high, we were in for another infusion of organized joy.

Softball as played by Detachment K bore little resemblance to the game conceived by Abner Doubleday. To start with, both infield and outfield crowded home plate to shorten the trip to the "dugout" once three reluctant batters waved at the pitcher three times and retired. On those rare occasions when a hit dribbled out to the infield, the game took on all aspects of dodge ball – or sometimes tag when players short on experience and throwing power raced among their teammates, determined to deliver the ball in person.

In a hasty pre-game conference, both sides agreed to start their batting order with the heaviest hitters. If one of them misguidedly connected and the ball flew into the surrounding underbrush so, too, did the entire outfield to return only after the game was called for what even the officers recognized as a certain lack of interest. Meanwhile the infield covered their positions in the best way possible, sprawled on the bases convinced – and correctly – the bottom of the batting order would never make a hit anyway.

With playtime over, we were whistled back into formation to head for the showers and home. Not quite. "Sergeant," bellowed the officer in charge, "have the company fall out and reform in groups of four, the ranking member to be in charge. Issue her a map and compass." Then, salting her language with such esoteric babble as "back azimuth," "oblique illumination," "coordinates," "hachures," "vectors" and "bench marks," she raced through what may still stand as the shortest map-reading refresher course on record. "In conclusion," she said, "you are to get back to camp by the quickest shortest route possible using only the tools at hand."

We were then dispatched to widely scattered sites within

a three-mile radius. The corporal steering our foursome took one look at her map and casually tossed it into the bushes: "So much for that 'tool at hand'; use it and we sure as hell won't be home by suppertime, maybe not even breakfast. It happens to be a quadrant of the reservation at Ft. Benning, Georgia – not Ft. Oglethorpe."

"So what do we do now, Corp?" someone asked.

"Improvise. One of the cadre told me there's a little lakeside amusement park over that way about a mile. What say we drive over there, have a few beers, take in the sights, and then head for home?"

"Great idea – but what if we get lost?"

"Absolutely no way. See that water tower in the distance. It's a little bit east northeast of camp. We just take a bead on it and keep walking."

"Great idea. But how come you know all that stuff?"

"Hey, that's why I'm a corporal."

After surviving what we considered the second battle of Chickamauga, we were treated to our first picnic, Army style – appropriate known in official circles as messing in the field. Its purpose: to acquaint us with eating implements that would feed us in the months to come, and the cooks with the preparation of menus on the move. Toward this end, each of us acquired a metal mess kit holding the three basic utensils – knife, fork and spoon – and pint-sized, kidney-shaped drinking cup snugged onto the canvas-cased canteen when not in use. The mess kit, properly assembled for use, vaguely resembled a pair of baby bed pans discounting the dividers in one half. Of the two parts, one was fairly stable being permanently hinged to a collapsible handle onto which the other balanced precariously in tandem to the first. Into both the unhappy cooks, charred by frequent encounters with eccentric kerosene stoves, tossed whatever bad dispositions and balky rolling kitchens produced.

Juggling food in one hand and a blistering cup of coffee in the other did not guarantee nourishment. Half the kit often jumped the track, the cup handle collapsed, and "messing in the field" often ended in messing up the field and ourselves.

By now, our scheduled two weeks of overseas training had

ended but still no port call. By popular command, we were extended for another week, or two, or whatever. Instructors coped with the delay by simply recycling the original program – with a few added attractions. Like packing 90 pounds of gear into a duffle bag designed to hold 50; practicing to splint and bandage without maiming (then being told to forget the whole thing because we'd probably just make a minor injury into a major one); falling and crawling undetected with shapes not designed to defy concealment; marching endless miles under what appeared to be back-breaking packs but which we usually bulked out with nothing weightier than a few dozen sanitary napkins. (A male trainee at Ft. Gordon achieved the same effect by stuffing his pack with inflated condoms until a suspicious sergeant upended the works across the path of a visiting delegation of DARs.) Our deception ended when one blithe spirit, resting her back from the assumed bends, not only straightened up but even skipped a few steps. After that, the sergeant flipped each pack before we hit the road.

To test our falling and crawling response, we frequently engaged during these marches in simulated air raids: a whistle, thrice tooted, warned us to scatter and take cover while a bored-looking Lieutenant with that ubiquitous clip board stood her ground clocking the time it took us to disappear. After two rather pitiful performances which she did not hesitate to mention, we redoubled our efforts on the next triple tweet, diving into the underbrush like scared hares, tucking our rumps as close to the good earth as female contours permitted. That is, all except one loner who dropped to all fours and then rebounded in what appeared to be one continuous motion.

"Down! Down! Down!!!" hollered the Lieutenant. "Don't you realize what we're practicing here is total war."

"Then, maybe ma'm, we should practice somewhere else. That's one granddaddy poison ivy patch your company's lying in."

A rather unruly stampede propelled us back to barracks where most of the next 24 hours was spent searching for signs of itching and inflammation which, happily, never appeared. So ended our instruction in the minor martial art of falling and crawling.

Meanwhile, the delay in our departure dragged into its second week – our fourth in the same set of grungy coveralls, the same towelless showers, the same drafty billets with their resident rat packs. The only oasis in this olive drab existence: the Post Exchange, probably antecedent of all the one-stop shops that clutter the countryside today. However, the PX had one distinct advantage over its latter-day clones: 3.2% beer, the only alcoholic beverage available to the lower grades - to which I seemed permanently attached – could be consumed on the premises; no ID required since the WAAC/WAC admitted no one below the age of 20.

Along with sandwiches, sodas, sundries, and several thousand needments of various descriptions – all priced to suit a soldier's pay – the PX stocked as perhaps its fastest moving item – rumor. Where else would anyone expect to hear the second front was about to open in Reykjavik, that Mrs. Roosevelt was poised to replace Hobby, that Ike had slapped Patton?

Had pollution been a serious concern in those days, the Oglethorpe PX might have drawn national attention. In a far corner, the bubbling juke box blared out such favorites as "I'm Walking The Floor Over You", "I Want To Be A Cowboy's Sweetheart", and No. 1 in that week's PX popularity poll – "I've Got Tears In My Ears Lying On My Back Crying Over You" – at a decibel level just about right for shattering crystal. The air, a vaporous mix of malt, shoe polish, and long-defunct cigarettes was barely breathable. Well before the lights blinked for closing time, every trash can overflowed with the discards of the loud-lunged crowd, spilling sodden cigarette packs, potato chip sacks, stale bread crusts, and butt-filled beer bottles across the room. Those contributing to the shambles prayed they wouldn't pull clean-up duty the next morning, but, in time, every mother's daughter of them did.

But even policing the PX was preferable to spending a woodsy night under canvas, an experience about as relaxing as an outing with Outward Bound.

The procedure for pop-tent pitching had been covered in a twenty-minute crash course early in our stay, with no time then or since for its practical application. Until now.

To biovac in the boonies, we first freighted ourselves with

enough miscellany to stock an Irish tinker's wagon: helmet, gas mask, canteen, mess kit, pistol belt, trench shovel, musette bag, blankets – and something called a shelter half which, when partnered with another of the same and properly coaxed aloft was meant to levitate into a tent for two little larger than a caret mark. Costumed for this camp out, individual identities dissolved into Ozian mutations somewhere between the Scarecrow and the Tin Man.

So ornamented, we staggered out into the north Georgia wilderness clanking the two miles to a rendezvous already awash with heavy rains. Adding to the joys of this outdoor experience: the cadre had forgotten the flashlights, and the ground around the site selected totally defied the digging of slit trenches. Whatever shallow runnels we managed to scratch in the stony soil ran full and furious, creating a primitive flush toilet, to be sure, but hardly what the Army intended.

After pairing us off – by the numbers, not by choice – a Sergeant set us to raising our tents, also by the numbers. One: roll out the halves. Two: button halves together. Three: insert pegs in bottom loops. Four: set poles fore and aft. Five: elevate tent. Six: drive in pegs. Seven: check for sag. Eight: start all over.

Around midnight the tents, improperly buttoned, inadequately pegged, and not ditched at all were officially declared habitable. This included any canvas six or more inches off the ground. The officer in-charge made a hurried inspection, turned the company over to her non-com, and wisely disappeared.

Within moments of her departure, a mini-monsoon roared through – collapsing even the lowliest of crawl space, sending a few shelters spinning off toward Chattanooga. My partner Weinerth and I managed by folding all four blankets into a mattress for two, wearing extra socks as mittens, using the tent as a poncho, and keeping all our clothes on for warmth. Through chattering teeth, she regaled me with stories of her lost youth in Chicopee, Mass., until the officer in charge, flushed with good health, reappeared the next morning to lead us, stumbling, back to barracks.

Hopeful signs of impending departure began appearing. Convoy officers assigned to nanny us to our destination wandered around sizing up their latest charges, while we underwent the granddaddy of all physical exams – from molars to metatarsals. Although little exceptional usually marks these revealing interludes which the Army then celebrated with some frequency, a female contract doctor who must have been close kin to Nurse Ratchet made this one memorable.

Peeling off her rubber gloves as she flopped into the chair beside me, she hailed the dentist then exploring my mouth: "Hey, Harry, listen to this. Eighty pelvics in an hour" as if Guinness was waiting to record her triumph. If the dentist's probe didn't make me jump, that bit of intelligence certainly did. Inevitably, she and I met again in her personal theater of operations – a string of eight unscreened tables which, leaving whimpers and worse in her wake, she covered as if wearing cleats. Obviously, she had slowed to catch her second wind; on me, she spent an entire minute gloves-to-gloves. No danger she'll ever be accused of wasting time at the orifice.

As a grand finale to this two-day "show and tell," a psychiatrist who, after hammering our patellae, asked only one question: "Do you like women?" In a totally woman's world, try answering that one. "No" means anti-social attitude; "Yes," suggests an all too friendly one.

Having exhausted our instructors as well as their ability to keep us amused, we were called out to attend a parade one afternoon in our usual dishabille. Not as participants, however, but rather to "paper the house." That is, we were herded into the shadows at the far end of the parade ground to bolster the training center's body count to impress some visiting Congressmen. Set apart to avoid embarrassing questions about our appearance and even our very existence which was meant to be "top secret," we slouched and skulked amid the pin oaks as our poster-perfect sisters-in-arms, a rather splendid sight, glided around the field, doing their star turn to a medley of Sousa marches.

Despite our protective coloring and unobtrusiveness, someone was bound to notice us.

Someone did.

During a lull in the music, the conversation of a couple who had found their way to our corner of the field floated to the fringes of our formation.

"Good Lord, what an odd-looking bunch that is," said the young lady, pointing us out to her escort. "What do you suppose those are?"

"Oh, they're prisoners, honey. Look! They're standing right in front of the guard house." Which, indeed, we were – although it wasn't in use as such at the time.

"But there're so many of them, Charlie. They couldn't all be as bad as the newspapers say. What do you suppose they're in for?"

"The usual, I guess. You know – drunkenness, insubordination, AWOL – probably prostitution."

Facelli, standing to my right, punched me in the ribs. "See! I told you so – there are career opportunities in the Army."

Actually, the expertise of our curbside companion was slightly askew: the commission of serious transgressions among members of the Corps was rather rare and no guard houses were maintained for those who erred; a discharge was the usual solution. For minor infractions, confinement to quarters was one of the few possible punishments, and even this need not be a hardship as I was about to learn.

Seven

We'll Be Seeing You

ALERTED FOR an early ship-out date a few days later, we were permitted a quick trip to the main post to make what were expected to be our last phone calls home. Lines were long, service slow, and the rest of the company was already standing retreat when I returned. After being thoroughly reprimanded for being late, I expected the matter to end there. But the officer in charge, who carried a swagger stick, and, reportedly, was as thin-skinned as cold cocoa, had other plans.

"You seem to have a little difficulty following orders," she barked, "so I'll give you some time to think things over. Confined to quarters until further notice." Having so decreed she promptly forgot I existed; had it been within her power, I'm sure she would have properly drummed me out of the corps, although slashing off my buttons might have proved an embarrassment to both of us – the only two attached to my coveralls, albeit precariously, were holding up the drop seat.

This time I obeyed her orders to the letter, languishing in the barracks, dining on smuggled rations, reading while others busied about, lying abed much of every day until it was almost pack-up time and we were truly headed out.

Through the doorway I could see the same officer, now known locally if not all too lovingly as Lt. Attica, listening to the report of the First Sergeant's roll call, the first anyone had mustered for several days:

"All accounted for, ma'm. Except Starbird."

"And where is Starbird?"

"She's in barracks, ma'm."

"Sick?"

"No, ma'm."

"Then why isn't she out here?"

"Confined to quarters, ma'm."

"By whose orders?"

"Yours, ma'm."

No one said "Let her out." No one said "All is forgiven." The Lieutenant left us in what could best be called high dudgeon, so without waiting for anyone's orders to do so, I resumed my rightful place among my fellow patriots.

I might have languished longer, but everything now pointed to our departure within the next day or two. The Legal Officer showed up to help us with our wills; those without the full $10,000 of GI insurance were encouraged, rather forcibly I thought, to take the max; in this pre-plastic age, toiletries were transferred to tin; the two-bit coveralls were returned – without a refund. And an enlisted instructor concentrated on teaching us the proper way to pack.

Now, civilian packing need not be scientific – the left-overs can always go UPS. No so for troops in transit; everything was shoehorned into that musette bag, little larger than a shoulder purse, and a cylindrical canvas duffle some three feet deep and about 18 inches in diameter. To make carrier and contents come out even, every item was rolled or folded to precise dimensions then wedged in exactly as prescribed on a large wall chart. What wouldn't fit in the first time was mangled and mashed until it did. Aided somewhat by the bouncing of butts of the heaviest WACs in the outfit.

Without our knowing it, the countdown for Ike's D-Day – June 6, 1944 – had already begun; now, in late May, ours had finally arrived. Laden and lumbering like the pack mules that preceded us onto this post, we headed downhill toward where our troop train panted for us, trying to look as menacing as possible as we passed the POW camp whose blond young giants in once-crisp tunics crowded the chain-link fence to serenade us.

"Hey, I know that song," said the woman marching beside me. "Not all the words, but it's something about wishing us luck and good hunting. Dammit, even the enemy doesn't take us seriously." She sulked all the way to the siding, but once there, everyone's spirit rose – we were, at last, headed somewhere. At this point, anywhere would do.

Despite the amount of tropic issue crammed into our baggage, most insisted we were eastbound. The train went west. Slowly. Or so it seemed until we crossed the Mississippi River the second day out. No stop before St. Louis provided platform space enough to stretch 400 pairs of legs, so we were pretty much anchored to the cars and seats assigned.

There's a common belief among the military that only nut cases volunteer. I disagree. It's always a gamble, of course, whether the special duty proves better or worse than the day's prescribed activities. Willing to chance it, I raised my hand when the call came.

"Good, private, you're on KP for the duration," the convoy officer informed me.

"The duration…?" I gulped. Perhaps I had been a little hasty.

"Of this trip," she added.

"What a jerk," commented one of our tour group, meaning me.

"My sentiments exactly," agreed another.

As it turned out – I drew the cushiest job aboard: no pots to scrub, no dishes to wash. Released from the confinement of an assigned seat and car and the boredom that appends thereto, I lurched the entire length of the train at will, delivering the box lunches that sustained us, collecting the trash they generated, then pitching the whole mess out of the sliding doors of a freight car to litter the countryside with the remnants of our passing.

A Harvey girl I was not.

When not engaged in these grueling official duties, I perched on a GI can in our kitchen car debating with Capt. Lawson, our convoy officer, the relative merits of my home state of Vermont vs. hers of Nebraska, through which we were then passing. Here, in this stark yet appealing part of the world, you can, on a clear day, see forever. And almost as far on a rainy one.

Line storms, gathering as tiny ink blots on the horizon miles away, prove the point. Spreading like Rorschach tests across a seemingly limitless landscape, they shade the few signs of settlement – an occasional farmhouse with no more than a tree or two, a single sentinel windmill – to their barest outlines, achieving a steel etching of magnificent proportions. And everywhere lightning, doing its best to add a little dazzle to a monochromatic masterpiece, resembles random chalk marks on a child's slate.

With all this unused space slipping by, someone was bound to remember our neglected bodies, ordering us out at every fuel- and water-stop to march about and practice a rather relaxed form of PT – pretty hot work when the only shade for miles was the WAC blocking your sunny side.

No matter how deserted a stop-over seemed upon arrival, within moments we were usually playing to a stand-up crowd, the local folk streaming by in wagon, pickup, and afoot to gawp at the best traveling show since the county fair.

Occasionally we de-trained at one of those vanishing vestiges of the age of steam – a real tank town: a few modest houses, a water tower with its pivoting pipe, coal chute and, if accessible by more than a cart track, probably a church and general store. Any shopkeeper along our route knew instant prosperity; in the few free moments between body-building and the whistle tooting us back aboard, we invaded like locusts, stripping his shelves of eatables, potables, postcards, and cigarettes while the more voracious shoppers among us – long denied an outlet for their natural urges – scooped up straw hats, red suspenders, and multicolored kerchiefs which Lawson, bless her, let them wear while beyond public view until the end of the line. Little did we know that even stranger items would soon clothe us.

No stop proved more gratifying and financially less demanding than little North Platte, Nebraska (pop: 13,500 at the time), an experience that forced me to cede extra points to Capt. Lawson in our ongoing interstate brag-fest.

Here, in the middle of cornhusker country – where clocks move back an hour and days go along at a farmer's pace – mothers and others for miles around had converted much of the Union Pacific's trackside depot into a joyous amalgam of covered-dish social, unrestricted service club, and top-of-the-line pig-out place. In the ten minutes it took there to refuel passing troop trains, the local ladies re-fueled everyone aboard with the bounty from their gardens, orchards, poultry yards, and kitchens. In the five years of its existence (1941-46), the North Platte canteen catered to more than 6 million members of the Armed Forces.

It was all sort of a grab and gulp affair, with an endless free offering of sandwiches, baked goods, fried chicken, hardboiled eggs and beverages along with unlimited carry-out cigarettes, candy bars, and reading materials. Everyone was encouraged to stoke up and stock up – for here lay living proof of why this corner of the nation was called America's heart-land.

By far the busiest table sagged beneath the weight of homemade frosted cakes being doled out to those claiming birthdays on that date. A certain amount of deception crept into these negotiations: when I asked a corporal if it really was his birthday, he replied – quite logically I thought – "If the British monarch can celebrate his birthday on any date he chooses, so can I."

On our fifth day out of Oglethorpe, we puffed uphill to Truckee on the California border then squealed down the sunset side of the Sierra Nevada into Camp Stoneman, our last stateside stop and one of those instant installations whose architect might have been a five-year-old with a set of Legos.

Called a staging area, about all it contributed to our military readiness was the ability to climb and descend a 40-foot cargo net without undue panic. Helmets must be worn but unbuckled, leading to the additional hazard of being rained on by falling headgear from above.

Those who benefited most from this experience: timid souls who froze halfway up, requiring rescue by two muscled Marines detailed for just that purpose. Our team finally put some points on the board when a Ground Force grunt in the climbing party ahead got height fright and two nimble WACs, out-racing his buddies, eased him back to earth.

Finally transition from wheel to keel transpired a few days later when we boated down the Sacramento River then across

San Pablo Bay to debark on a San Francisco fish wharf beside a great grey ghost of a ship which, before donning war paint, rode tranquil seas to and from Honolulu as the virginally white, ultramodern SS Matsonia.

Her peacetime role – strictly R&R for the leisure class – found expression in a 1940's Matson Line brochure bootlegged to me by one of the Merchant Marine crew:

> *"Sail the scenic Pacific in a gay, bright 'city afloat'!*
> *Romance and adventure await you where the lazy trade winds*
> *ruffle the azure waters and calm your jagged nerves. The cruise*
> *begins at the gangplank...your luggage precedes you without*
> *you lifting a finger..."*

Bowed under everything we owned, we schlepped aboard to the ragged beat of a 5-piece band playing *Do Nothing 'Till You Hear From Me*, preferring the far pleasanter music of welcoming whistles from some 3,000 GIs already aboard.

Besides this appreciative audience, departure offered other compensations: a 20% pay increase when we hit the gangplank; Red Cross ditty bags inadvertently scrambled in the giving – ours with razors and aftershave; theirs with lipstick and sanitary napkins.

That pre-war brochure suggested other delights were at hand:

> *"Your bedroom is your retreat where you rest between gaieties*
> *with every facility as near as the phone on your night table."*

Room assignments pretty much followed the chain of command – the higher the rank the loftier its accommodations. Under this arrangement, officers occupied A deck and above; enlisted men, B and C decks. D deck housed the "dining saloons;" E deck, wedged between galley and engine room and encapsulating the exhaust of both, the enlisted WACs. Strategically located at the torpedo line and as far as possible from the lifeboats, it was obvious who'd be singing "Nearer My God To Thee" if the ship went down.

WACs of the PFC persuasion were stacked six to a 12'x10' priest hole, where no more than two once traveled, in a stateroom scene reminiscent of the Marx Brothers' flick, *A Night At The Opera.* Or fourteen Dartmouth students in a phone booth.

Within our space – sort of fitted around an outside cabin – we shared a sink large enough for a single sock, a spigot ejecting only cold salt water, a sliver of soap, a consumptive fan, and two triple-decker bunks that would cause a mole claustrophobia. Perhaps to create the illusion of "rm ocn vu" a shoulder-wide slot projected, like a pump handle, another 12 feed to the ship's hull, revealing a porthole not only blacked out but welded shut.

Having been in grade a week longer than any other one-striper on our corridor, I was put in charge of the lot – 36 WACs in six rooms. This mostly involved trying to keep their spirits up and rations down. To achieve the latter, I fetched saltines and bananas from the mess hall/saloon to quiet their nausea and, since the communal head lay beyond easy reach of the queasy, emptied their helmets when this failed.

On deck, inexperienced voyagers, urged not to stare at the undulating horizon, did just that, soon finding the stuffy staterooms below preferable to disgracing themselves in the fresh air above. GIs one deck down applauded their decision. I did not. Don't ever talk to me about the loneliness of command.

Back to that brochure:

"The deck is your campus and playground."

Not exactly!

Whistled topside for one last pulsating glimpse of the Golden Gate, the cruise began on a promising note with all WACs regardless of rank mingling freely on the sun deck with all officers regardless of sex. A certain camaraderie developed immediately between male officers and enlisted women who, on average, were younger and a bit livelier than their commissioned counterparts. This arrangement was doomed from the very start.

By the next day, our "playground" had shrunk to the starboard side of the sun deck during rigidly enforced hours with absolutely no fraternization. Still, some of the more daring managed to slip across the "international date line" and into alien territory after dark. This would never do.

By the fourth day, our "campus" was further compacted to just half the fan tail with a Marine standing guard in the "no man's land" between them and us, and our time aloft limited to even shorter, closer-supervised shifts. Dreams of sunning ourselves across the azure Pacific soon dwindled; our sliver of the deck was to be utilized primarily to keep us fit.

Actually, the Matsonia was ill-suited for such purpose having lost almost forty feet from her original length shortly after launching. To speed her return to trans-Pacific service, repairs consisted mainly of lopping off the damaged end and sealing it with a new stern. Consequently, her natural roll became more pronounced, upending more than one body builder among us even on fairly quiet seas.

Calisthenics couldn't possibly survive under these conditions but before being abandoned, they allowed me one of life's major victories – my first and final push up. Laced into a bulky Mae West life jacket, its chest touched down while my own, inside, remained several inches above deck. I say it counted – I never came that close again.

In all important ways, the Matsonia made an excellent transport. Traveling without convoy, which at 22 knots cruising speed she could outrun anyway, she bee-lined from America to the Antipodes in just over 13 days, ferrying those 3,000 troops plus us in accommodations designed for 577 paying passengers, 365 crew. During our crossing, no one died, fell overboard, wed, went underfed or attracted hostile attention. (Several years later while living in Honolulu, I claimed press credentials I didn't have, went aboard her again for a nostalgic walk-about, hugged the Captain, and praised the elegance of her post-war refit which made even my old quarters – minus bodies, baggage, and extra bunks – look almost livable.)

Where pre-war passengers played shuffleboard and popped away at clay pigeons, gun crews rumbled off a few rounds each day just to keep their hand in. But even as the Southern Cross brightened night skies and we lost a day in all that vastness, certain participants in my destination derby refused to even believe the Captain when he announced we were headed for Australia; claiming the trip was just a diversionary tactic, they refused to pay up until they saw their first kangaroo. Both of which they eventually did.

Probably our most entertaining fellow-travelers: schools of flying fish that frolicked in the bow's big curl or planed along beside us like so many well-skipped stones. After dark, they still kept us company, their torpedo bodies and phosphorescent fins flaming more brilliantly, it seemed to us, than any number of lighted cigarettes denied during blackout. Obviously, the enemy toiled elsewhere those nights.

"Sports, vivid, varied, vibrant, are yours..."

Other than fish-spotting and star-gazing, about our only other open air occupation was swapping banter with the lads on the deck below while the Marine MPs shadowed our every move to prevent closer contact.

"Geez, Sarge," complained one Semper Fi, "stick 'em in fatigues, helmets, and Mae Wests, how'm I meant to tell the he's from the she's?"

"Look at their feet, dummy. Or if they wiggle when they walk, chances are they're female." The sergeant paused, "but then again, maybe not."

Someone guessed wrong somewhere: when we arrived in Brisbane, two couples announced their betrothal and a goodly number of WACs wore items of GI clothing they had mysteriously acquired en route.

During the trip, not all distractions originated on the fan tail. Even after that all-purpose physical at Oglethorpe, a pretty thorough look-see at Stoneman, some sadist – ignoring our continuous lack of opportunity since – decided to repeat the pelvic poke in mid-ocean.

The doctor who arrived at our cabin was slightly over five feet tall. He couldn't possibly examine a patient in the upper bunk, to do so on the lower would bring him to his knees. So each of us, in turn, crawled into the middle bunk, whimpering a little each time the rolling ship upset the doctor's aim.

This same tipsy motion added a certain zest to the performance of a USO troupe that bounded out of nowhere late in the cruise to entertain, in ascending order, everyone aboard. By the time they reached the top deck and us among others, unruly winds and rockabye waves let us know they were not the Flying Wollandas. But they carried on valiantly in the finest theater tradition, juggling manfully as props shot seaward, leaping into human pyramids pared down by several tiers, and, in a rather spectacular finale, saving a unicyclist doing an improbably manual-of-arms from being blown over the side. Despite thunderous applause, they refused an encore.

Packing up took little effort. We'd never had room to unpack. By the time we entered the looping Brisbane River for the last 13 miles to the city's Hamilton Dock the sun deck suddenly became open space again; mingling was barely monitored.

Eight

The South Pacific

OUR WELCOME, unlike our stateside farewell, dazzled: a fully Army band resplendent in white gloves, puttees, fourragères – the kind of thing the military does when it's trying to impress. An honor guard. Flags flying all over the place. Cameras whirring. Hey, this was more like it.

Debarking the S.S. Matsonia in Brisbane, Australia, June 1944.

The arrow points to Starbird.

Then, in a blaze of ribbons, Mr. Big himself – Douglas A. MacArthur – trailing bird colonels like a meteor, wearing enough "scrambled eggs" on his garrison cap to make an omelet. Moving in close, he greeted the first to land – not one of our crowd but the far more illustrious Australian Prime Minister John J. Curtain who had booked passage on the same ship!

Back in March 1942, MacArthur had set up his Far East Command in Brisbane preparatory to launching a counter-offensive against the Japanese colossus which earlier that year controlled everything from Wake Island to Burma, from Sitka in the Aleutians through all of modern-day Indonesia, Vietnam, and a healthy chunk of China.

This included Buna on the north coast of Papua New Guinea and within easy striking distance of mainland Australia. The Japanese had targeted Port Moresby on the south shore as their next objective which would have brought them even closer. But for the Australian foot soldier – the indomitable digger – they might have made it.

Between Buna and Moresby lay the formidable Owen Stanley Mountains; across them threaded the Kokoda Trail, a precipitous footpath slimmed with near-constant rains, its jungled growth alive with every virulent disease in the tropical lexicon. Yet the diggers scrambled up and over, securing Moresby, retaking Buna. (I find this worth repeating not only for the heroics involved because Pathe's scenes of the operation sent me off to the Recruiting Office in the first place.)

Moving General Headquarters (GHQ) to Brisbane not only thwarted the threat to Australia but provided the Allies a springboard for recapturing the Solomons, Gilberts, most of New Guinea and various smaller satellite island groups before WACs ever arrived on the scene. In doing so, we brought to over 1,000 (out of an eventual 5,500) the number of us serving in the Southwest Pacific Area (SWPA), all of them in Brisbane except 276 of the first shipment now staffing a Postal Unit in Moresby, where letters passing through their conscientious censorship often emerged looking as lacy as music rolls from an old player piano.

We all envied Moresby's "Guinea hens" being "up North" (anywhere from Toowoomba to Tokyo) became the Holy Grail of SWPA WACdom. To beat Army nurses to a forward location, usually and rightfully an impossibility - was our challenge; to follow the Red Cross a disgrace.

With landing also came parting: now being almost joined at the hip, the detachment split, some going off to the US Army Services of Supply (USASOS) at Victoria Park, the rest destined for the US Army Forces Far East (USAFFE) which set up housekeeping in Yeronga Park some ten miles south of the city. Although many WACs were officially attached to lesser commands, MacArthur, while utilizing their skills in GHQ, refused to acknowledge them as members of his staff; they were detailed for duty there but not actually assigned until months later. In the meantime, they were carried on the rolls and wore the patch of USAFFE.

Within a few days after arrival, a classification officer summoned us for a qualification check and job assignment. Certainly after a friendly discussion of my attributes, I'd be doing something more glamorous than clerk work.

"Your typing speed?" the interviewer asked.

"Sixty words a minute, ma'm. But I'm awfully good at..."

"Next!"

So much for Army classification.

In the divvy-up of incoming WACs, a long-time – by Army reckoning – associate of mine named Weinerth, moving over to USASOS, had the great good fortune to end up employed by then-Colonel A. Robert Ginsburgh whose fame preceded him into the Pacific not only as a superb officer but also as a star player in a great story still in circulation today.

The time: late 1941. The place: Washington, D.C. Pearl Harbor had just happened and two starchy Georgetown matrons, anxious to boost troop morale (as the Cambridge ladies did later) called the Secretary of War's office to invite two GIs to Sunday dinner.

"But, of course," said the voice at the Georgetown end of the phone, "no Jews."

The day arrived and so did the guests. The door opened on

two of the biggest, beamingest black soldiers to be found in the District of Columbia.

"Oh, no…" stammered one of the dowagers, "…there must be some mistake."

"Oh, no, ma'm," said one of the men, "Col. Ginsburgh, he don't make no mistakes."

Whereas Weinerth, obviously, drew a nifty boss, I lucked into a lemon.

True, to get overseas I had elected to go clerk class, convinced I could wrangle an early transfer. But with no possibilities immediately in sight I went to work at USAFFE headquarters filing 3x5-inch cards on the dead, wounded, and injured, the difference between the latter two being whether it was combat or non-combat incurred.

The job consisted mainly of collecting non-classified details on deaths and to maintain progress reports on the disabled so the nearest of kin could be kept informed. My major task, however: plotting an early escape.

By far the greatest irritant on this assignment: serving under a branch chief (a position he strove to take literally) who, in acquiring an all-enlisted WAC staff, thought he had inherited a harem with whom he could play pasha.

Like all Army warrant officers, he occupied a unique position in the chain-of-command: he could fraternize with any rank he chose – officer or enlisted. But since we were all enlisted WACs, appearing publicly with any of us might tarnish his self image as a respected member of the officer class. So this little charmer tried to set up back-alley deals: you bring the body, he'd bring the booze. His revenge for rejection: threats of negative efficiency ratings, delayed promotions, blocked transfers. To those of us still around when charges of sexual harassment at Aberdeen Proving Grounds hit the headlines in 1996, this was very old news.

By contrast – while attempting one morning to let a General precede me onto an elevator, I resorted to what became known as the Queen Street shuffle: into the car, out of the car, glide to the side then – if all else failed – take the next car up. The General stood his ground behind me, finally ordered me aboard saying, "After you, private. I was a gentleman before I was an officer."

For reasons never explained, the Casualty Section came equipped with a then-modern miracle called the McBee System, the cave art of computers. Designed primarily to speed up the selection of personnel for specific jobs, the contraption consisted of a bunch of metal skewers, a lidless box about the size of a child's coffin, and any number of cards (do not bend, fold or spindle) punched like a train ticket to indicate a candidate's qualifications. By impaling cards on the skewers, slotting skewers on the box rim, and vigorously shaking the whole mess, eligibles would sift to the bottom. Discounting a certain margin for error. So while it wasn't Big Blue, at least it was never "down."

Having mastered the office's file card flow, I was – additionally – given the problem mail to answer: correspondence generated by suicides, self-inflicted wounds – and stupidity. Try explaining to a wife back home that her husband has blown away some irreplaceable assets by tossing a lighted cigarette down the latrine, an empty but still flammable oil drum on which he was sitting at the time. Or why this hadn't earned him a Purple Heart.

My corresponding would later assume a certain cachet when it was expanded to include MacArthur's condolence letters. Not for the most senior KIAs which he supposedly composed himself (as the one my sister received a year later)[8] but for the echelon below. Neither skill ever impressed any of my future employers.

While workdays dragged, living among the Aussies in a country as fascinating as any on earth was well worth the trip.

I had always imagined the land down under as being a Jurassic Park sort of place or looking like an illustration from one of those early geography books that shoed a primeval forest before it fossilized to coal: trees of great girth and height, ferns and termite mounds as high as some houses, vines Tarzan could swing on. These existed then and still do. So, too, did places like Brisbane, an outpost of Empire teetering on the brink of what it would become: a thriving port city of more than a million population, manufacturing center, retail outlet for much of northeast Australia,

---

8   Starbird's brother-in-law, Brig. Gen. James Leo Dalton II was killed in action May 16, 1945 at Balete Pass, Luzon Island, Philippines. In his honor, Balete Pass was renamed Dalton Pass. Dalton and Starbird's brother, Alfred Dodd Starbird, both graduated from West Point in '33.

and gateway to two of the continent's major tourist attractions –
its beach-studded Gold Coast and the Great Barrier Reef.

The city's commercial hub revolved around a rather loose
collection of low, multi-storied buildings dominated by the
towering city hall, roofed sidewalks, pushcart vendors, news
kiosks, Toonerville trolley transportation, and traffic moving in the
wrong direction. Clumped around light poles, off-duty military
types hawked chances of everything from doll carriages to seeing
eye dogs, the proceeds earmarked for some charitable cause
connected to the war effort.

Most pedestrians wore uniforms but in such a mob scene,
military courtesy had become a little lax. Lacking elbow room to
sling a salute, no one much even tried. Besides, few Yanks knew a
pip from a polyp, and the laid-back Aussies couldn't care less.

Encounters between GIs and WACs further impeded traffic.
Negotiations usually opened with "Where ya from, WAC?"
followed, in many cases with, "Do us a favor, will ya – just please
say cheese?" Which seemed a ridiculous request, until we realized
that local dentists favored pliers over preservation, and gold front
teeth or none at all. The boys from back home just wanted to
admire again an unblemished smile, American style.

Around the city's inner core clung a residential carapace of
neat bungalows perched on stilts (to cool inside and keep pests
outside) and screened from the street by near-continuous Tom
Sawyer type fence along which school boys still rattled their sticks.
In fact, much of the Brisbane scene suggested a Mark Twain sort
of town updated to about 1910.

But given the season, few U.S. counterparts of any period could
claim such flamboyant color. Even in winter, yards, trees, and
hedges flamed with blossoms; poinsettias most of us only knew
as potted plants exploded in hip-high profusion around almost
every doorway.

With cheeks almost as red, kids barefoot and appropriately
uniformed pedaled to school wearing back-pack book bags,
a sensible style it would take U.S. students another decade to
adopt.

Ignoring the cold that hovered only a few degrees above
freezing, the indomitable digger strode along in scanty shorts

as if looking for Livingston; his broad-brimmed campaign hat clipped up on one side suiting him to perfection. Yet, somehow, the knockoff now affected by the U.S. Army drill sergeant makes him/her look like a grouchy road company d'Artagnan – without the plume.

We felt immediately at home in Brisbane – largely because Aussies usually empathized with Americans and vice versa. After all, why not? Mother England birthed us both. As a result, we shared a common language – well, sort of. Learning the lyrics to "Waltzing Matilda" did not necessarily mean we understood them. Or why the many signs reading *Casket Closing* referred to the lottery, not the mortuary.

Any naturally we felt friendly toward a country that constantly coined ear-catching words for a distinctive vocabulary already more expressive than most; that preserved such euphonious aboriginal place names as Indooroophilly, Coolangata, and Murwillumbah (as we have Mississippi, Okefenokee, Menominee, etc.); that maintained such a Noah's Ark of endearing animals; at one time there were almost as many WAC-cuddling-koala pictures in circulation as those of Betty Grable's legs.

About a half-hour's commute by Clayfield tram from downtown Brisbane lay our billeting area at Yeronga Park, an orderly arrangement of unpaved pathways stitching together rows of six-person huts, bucket-bottom privies, open-air showers, and a few of the more usual amenities of the Army's standard home away from home. Our living quarters, as minimally furnished as a nun's, provided each of us with a metal wall locker and a cot – single on each side of the doorway, two double deckers in tandem across the rear wall – recreating the snug coziness of the Matsonia's E level cabins.

Ventilation pretty much depended on the position of each cabin's four swing-out shutters which, when raised simultaneously, created the impression that the whole compound was taxiing for take-off. Regulating heat was no problem – there simply wasn't any. Except in a few non-com huts equipped with a lethal weapon called a Brisbane heater, a strip of stove pipe enclosing a kerosene-soaked wick. The only way to counter its stifling exhaust when lit: open the door and every window – or toss the thing outside, either one a self-defeating exercise.

WAC Billets, Yeronga Park, Brisbane, Australia.

No one had mentioned that winter came early in these latitudes – six months early to be exact. Believing this a tropical climate (Brisbane is about as far south of the Equator as Havana, Cuba, is north of it) we expected to go immediately into suntans – and stay there. Instead we went immediately into everything we could muster, often wearing to bed flannel pajamas, overcoat, knit cap, sweater, and gloves under six wool blankets, the Army's answer for central heating.

The mercury set with the sun: Brisbaners may claim a mean low temperature of only 45 degrees F. in winter; to us it felt a whole lot meaner. Especially in the latrine area. Here, a pail under a wooden shelf sculpted to fit the butt served as a commode, a primitive arrangement providing easy access for the bucket brigade (thankfully an "outsourced" service) and any artic updrafts that passed that way.

It took a stout heart, firm will, and reliable flashlight to drive anyone to the showers after dark; sandwiched between scalding spray and icy winds, I felt like a baked Alaska. Wearing helmet liners for shower caps and shrouded in steam, we strongly resembled a corps de ballet of mushrooms performing "Swan Lake" in hell.

Given the turn-around time to town and back, bed check at 11:00 p.m. (2300 if you prefer), and limited leisure, much of our off-duty life revolved around the Yeronga scene. Once a month, we spent an entire day there fulfilling the private's recurrent obligation – KP.

Those tardy for the 5 a.m. sign-in rated the crummiest jobs; under this arrangement I regularly drew the grease trap and wash-tub tending. Stateside, a grease trap is a relatively simple device, usually a cruddy little glop-catcher under the sink, gagging to hang around but not too tough to keep clean. The Yeronga model, on the other hand, was easily the size of a Jacuzzi into which I descended in hip boots and gas mask (proving it had some use) to ladle a sort of primordial ooze into shoulder-level buckets until the Mess Sergeant approved the results.

This done, I joined another hapless soul to empty, scrub, refill, and stoke the pokey fire beneath three split oil drums holding water for mess-kit wash up. Into the first we whittled flakes from a wedge of GI soap, probably the only gold bars we'd ever earn. Bailing and refilling these tubs three times a day mangled most muscles; chopping discarded crates into firewood with a meat cleaver took care of the rest.

In a weird way, pulling KP did remind me of home: Blodgett ovens and Edlund can openers, fixtures for most mess halls, were made in Burlington, Vermont, and I had written glowing advertising copy for both. Now, crawling into the ovens to clean them; working the can openers until I slung blood with each salute, I decided that, in practice, neither seemed quite the joy my ads implied.

The thing I minded most about Yeronga KP, the day it arrived so, too, did my monthly cramps. The First Sergeant refused to accept this as sufficient reason to revise her roster so the double trouble went on...and on...

One particularly painful evening, I shoved my serving spoon

into the hands of an unappreciative co-worker and staggered over to the dispensary, a brood hen of a building squatting on the far side of an intended but unused drill field as grassless and hard packed as a chicken yard. Its custodian, and elderly unwed country doctor who must have wondered how he ended up with an all-female practice a hemisphere from home (as did we) treated all minor ailments with the Army's "wonder" drug, APCs[9]; for anything more serious or mysterious, he administered straight Codeine, not my drug of choice. Probably because menstrual cramps were as much a mystery to him as me, he doubled the dose, making sure I downed both pills. Had anyone mentioned PMS in those days, he as well as we would have thought it a reference to the Provost Marshal's Section.

I have absolutely no recollection of re-crossing the drill field then piling face down and miraculously unscathed into a ten-foot stack of splintered food crates as nail-infested as a fakir's bed.

Two of my hut mates found me there and dragged me home. "God takes care of drunks and children..." I heard one of the say as I groggily came back into focus.

"She's not drunk, I tell you," said Dodie Young of the cot next to mine. "How could she be? No Private First Class could afford that much booze on her own. And she doesn't have the rank to get into a club where she could buy on the cheap."

Which was indeed the case. Membership in enlisted clubs was based on the caste system: corporals had theirs, sergeant society theirs, the two sometimes combining into a Non-commissioned Officers Club. Those of us at the bottom of the pecking order had neither a post PX nor our own spa in town as did the non-coms who could stock their bars and themselves from a liberal liquor ration. But what privates and PFCs did have was a monthly allotment of beer collected in kegs in the mess hall cooler until enough accumulated to launch a one-night revel, upper graders excluded.

Given the alcoholic content of Aussie beer – a rousing 12% or so to the PX's paltry 3.2% - and its near-continuous flow from

---

9   APC tablets were a combination of Aspirin, Phenacetin and Caffeine, used as a headache remedy. Phenacetin products were pulled from the market in 1983 by the FDA, due to "a high potential for harm to the kidneys."

generous pint-size canteen cups, the effect was about the same as being kicked by a kangaroo. Or so it proved for the uninitiated – a New Guinea-bound shipment of 80 WACs who, after a month at sea and no knowledge of native alchemy, stopped over with us for a few days and joined in one of these friendly romps. Words of warning did no good; it had been a long, dry voyage. For them, the day room lights blinked out early as they fell about everywhere but in bed. We were still picking them out of the bushes at reveille the next morning.

And while we're on this subject…

Aussies, among the world's most accomplished drinkers, tolerated some weird rules then (and still do) to retain this reputation. In 1944, pubs opened at odd intervals, usually served only an hour or two before locking up again and, because of shortages in popular brands, often switched to less agreeable spirits without warning.

Fearful of missing a moment of opportunity, the thirsty began assembling near our Queen Street offices by mid-afternoon determined to be the first out of the starting gate when it opened. Man by man, the crowd grew in size and impatience, blocking the sidewalk, spilling over the curb, eventually forcing passersby into the roadway.

Detouring around them after work often made me miss my tram; one day I decided to play through. Inching between a rising tide of tipplers and their objective, I was swept inside as the doors flew apart, carried effortlessly the length of the barroom, found my footing again practically in the arms of the publican.

Well, since I was there anyway…

Pulling out a fistful of shillings, I started to give my order.

"Sorry, miss," said mine host, "we don't serve ladies. Appreciate your dropping by, though. G'day."

I like to think it was nothing personal, just another silly down under drinking rule. It was true, however, that our arrival in the Antipodes was not universally applauded, the most vocal dissenters being some 20,000 Australians – most of them women – who had gone to work for the U.S. Army in the very jobs we were meant to fill – clerks, telephone operators, stenographers, chauffeurs. Not only were they paid above local scale but, having lost a significant percentage of their marriage-age men at Tobruk, Greece, Crete, and Malaya, US employment offered the easiest access to a fresh supply of males.

Attachments formed; it was hoped in some lofty quarters that the local-hire ladies would accompany US troops as they moved North. When Australian authorities prohibited any such out-migration, three American generals circumvented the proscription by declaring their favored civilian help – 1 British, 2 Australian – absolutely essential to the war effort and had them directly commissioned in the Women's Army Corps, a captain and two lieutenants. (The captain was particularly essential – by day she ran the officers' liquor locker.)

These shenanigans, vehemently opposed by Col. Hobby, were finalized just before the first WAC detachment landed in SWPA in May of 1944. She argued – one colonel against three generals – that such a travesty would demean the role of women in forward areas and undermine her troops' morale. It did both!

Naturally, the news still raged when our contingent, the second, arrived; at Yeronga we joined with those already in residence in a protest meeting our company officers, who shared our sentiments, chose to ignore. This loud and undisciplined rabble proposed to bring our resentment to the serious attention of the Inspector General's office, the closest the Army comes to an ombudsman. But how? Even more than six hundred enlisted WACs could hardly be expected to outmaneuver three generals.

"Hey, it's a cinch," said Walsh, the musical maven from Ad School who had preceded me to Yeronga. "We'll all just march in tomorrow and cancel our E-bond allotments. Betcha that'll bring them running."

We did – and they did in rather impressive numbers. We couldn't reverse the appointments or the damage done in making them nor would we reverse our position in bond-buying until assured that no more foreign nationals – generals' pets or no – would be commissioned. Our bargaining power had limitations, however; using the precedent set in SWPA, General Eisenhower had his British driver Kay Summersby made a WAC lieutenant. That, as far as I know, was the end of such appointments.

Nine

"Somewhere in the South Pacific"

THE MOVEMENT of WACs to New Guinea was beginning to escalate – more to Moresby, others breaking new ground at Oro Bay and Hollandia on the Dutch half of New Guinea which, incidentally, is the largest island in the world next to Greenland. Lt. Velma "Pat" Griffith, a Hoosier of great good humor and press savvy served as the only public relations officer for several thousand WACs scattered over an area about the size of Western Europe. Without her, the war would have seemed much longer – and probably would have been.

It was finally conceded that Pat deserved an enlisted assistant, and, in looking over the field, she decided that no one was more convincingly enlisted than I. The job was mine but I'd be stalled at Yeronga while she winged off to Hollandia to prepare a place for me. In the interim, she suggested I make myself useful to a cadre lieutenant named Opgrand who hadn't the slightest idea what to do with me.

Lacking direction, I cranked out hometown releases on the whole rear echelon which, measured in line count, produced my greatest body of work ever.

Unofficially, I had also become the resident ghost writer of those let-down letters known as "dear Johns." With such a plethora of escorts close at hand, a number of my camp mates decided to terminate earlier alliances with gentle words they felt unable to express. Thus I became proxy pen pal, trying to break off relationships through some of the most creative work I have ever done. Except, possibly, expense accounts in my later life.

About this time, a lurid domestic journal called *Truth* was establishing a far from truthful predecessor for what the States would later know as the supermarket tabloid. WACs did not escape attention.

Its pages screeched the plight of war-weary diggers – liberated, evacuated, or rotated home – finding the girls they left behind occupied with an inexhaustible supply of Yanks. *Truth* claimed WACs were forbidden to date diggers and, given the availability of their own countrymen, wouldn't if they could. First part: false; second part: probably true.

The accusation should have been ignored. Instead, someone up the chain of command decided to make peace, not war, by committing four of us to an enchanted evening with four of them. And Opgrand finally found a use for me; I would chair this allied assignation.

Tarted up in A uniforms and jeep-lifted to a deserted and darkening stretch of Brisbane docklands, we joined our escorts aboard a launch that looked like the last out of Dunkirk. Casting off for what we anticipated as a leisurely river cruise, the boatman steered to midstream, dropped anchor, curled up over the wheel and promptly went to sleep.

At this point, we began to doubt the efficacy of détente. Displaying our best boarding school manners, we enthused over the picnic supper laid out on the cabin roof, then stuffed ourselves, ever so slowly, with its bounty (excluding the Marmite.) We admired the beverage choice (beer, gin, no mixes) and politely asked for water.

Down to our last time-killing ploy, conversation, we talked long, enthusiastically, and without a whit of real knowledge about war strategy, Australian football, Labor Party politics, heroics at Gallipoli, and cricket. Despite the bone-chilling cold, we steadfastly stressed our preference for the bracing open air over the warm and cozy cabin below into which one of our hosts optimistically disappeared to plump the pillows on two couches.

His buddies, no grammarians to start with, were soon ending every sentence with a proposition.

Anticipating hand-to-hand combat, I yelled at the boatman to please put us ashore.

To a man, the Aussies bellowed back "Don't you do it, mite."

I repeated the request.

The answer remained the same.

Things were getting a little hairy. Trying one last gambit, I stood on the bow in my stocking feet and announced that if we didn't dock immediately, I was swimming in. My loyal comrades began to remove their shoes.

The boatman finally realized we might be serious; lacking the muscle or enthusiasm to hook us back aboard, he rumbled up to wharf, dropping us unceremoniously in yet another unpeopled patch of waterfront. Without comment or backward glance, the Aussies scooped up their bottles and disappeared down the hatch leaving us to fend afoot on unfamiliar terrain still some ten miles from camp. With the river between.

We wandered an hour before locating one of its two bridges, another hour before sighting human habitation, the best part of another to snare a reluctant cabbie and reach home. As we paid off the driver, the CQ (Charge of Quarters) exploded out of the orderly room in full cry: "You really tore it this time. You know how late it is – 0200, that's how late. You missed bed check. The duty officer's steaming. Report at 0700 for disciplinary action."

Four middle fingers unfurled in a salute befitting the occasion.

After this little romp on the river, the simple pleasures of camp life seemed even more appealing. The occasional movie that came our way - regardless of plot, players or production date - always drew a full house. The movie house was actually the day room - providing a few scattered folding funeral chairs and a new development in theater seating: the movable front row. After chairs filled, later arrivals, cocooned in blankets, squatted squaw-fashion on the floor, inching ever forward. By the tame the Pathe rooster crowed, the first row had traveled to within six inches of the screen.

Once house lights dimmed, audience participation robbed

comedians of their punch lines, heckled screen lovers in their most intimate moments, warned of impending dangers well before they happened.

The operator, usually a reluctant innocent recruited from our ranks, often added to the confusion by threading the film upside down, running reels out of sequence, or letting the projector overheat, toasting some of the more torrid footage beyond recognition.

The blame was not totally hers: films usually arrived already suffering from battle fatigue, patched and scratched like a luckless tom cat, frequently and imperfectly spliced. Sunny beaches seemed shrouded in London fog, actors walked through walls, lips didn't always synch with sound. Given breakdowns and, later, red alerts, blackouts and sudden cloud bursts, few films ran without major interruptions. After three false starts – in Australia, New Guinea, and the Philippines – I finally saw *Laura* uninterrupted and in its entirety, last year. On television.

For the hardier among us, live entertainment lay just beyond the fence separating our camp from the men's next door, a regular stop on the USO circuit. As we straddled the 8-foot divider or balanced precariously on empty cartons piled against it, an emcee in the hazy distance recycled *Joe Miller's Joke Book* while acrobats flipped, magicians bewildered, hoofers shuffled and no one had to tell us what happened to vaudeville.

Along with a tuneless piano, some year-old copies of *Good Housekeeping* and an occasional keg of beer, the day room housed the only public telephone in the compound, which, after word of our arrival, rang incessantly. Anyone inclined to answer merely lifted the receiver, said "she's gone North" and hung up. Which was probably true: departures in that direction had reduced our numbers to near-company strength: I might well be the one to turn off the lights and carry out the flag.

When the bulletin board announced the reopening of Officer Candidate School (OCS) back in the states for early 1945, ennui impelled me to apply. A personal interview in full summer uniform was part of the drill. To prepare for this solemn occasion, I sent my suntans off to a local laundress and for something slightly less than $10 she returned them starched stiffer than a hoe blade. Setting aside the skirt to preserve its pristine press, I blitzed my insignia, retied my tie five times, combed my hair, buttoned myself into my blouse and marched forth to meet my destiny. Fortunately, I met the gate guard first who called attention to one slight oversight: lacking a full length mirror (or any size for that matter) to assess my overall appearance, I was headed downtown without my skirt.

The year was slipping into September, deadline for mailing Christmas packages back to the home folks. Shopping in wartime Brisbane meant facing shortages of just about everything including someone to handle a purchase: if stores weren't closed for a bank holiday, the sales help was taking a tea break.

Having tried unsuccessfully to buy one of those English-type backpack book bags for a school-aged niece, I agreed when a Yeronga workman offered to make me one. He turned out a beauty – squarish, sturdy, and elegantly fashioned in genuine kangaroo skin. One small drawback: it was made of untanned leather and smelled worse than a fertilizer factory. Expecting fresh air to cure the problem, I hung it on our hut door until everyone inside threatened to move me outside. I then switched it to a nail at the back of the latrine, the one place I was sure no one would notice. Even the bucket-dumper complained. In desperation, I hooked it over the fence behind the men's camp whose occupants beat the bushes for days searching for something long dead. Present day patrons of Yeronga Park may still be looking.

The exodus of WACs from Australia continued, most moving by air. But a contingent from Victoria Park took a more leisurely trip by ship. Feeling his women had suffered press neglect, Col. Ginsburgh urged me to come out for the send-off and give it some coverage. For sheer entertainment, the embarkation ranked right up there with the Marx brothers.

After a long line of WACs filled up the gangplank, crowding the rail for final farewells to practically nobody but me, one particularly buxom lass on whom all eyes seemed focused kept crossing her arms modestly to conceal her natural endowment.

Even from the dock I noticed her bosom heaving at an unnatural cadence Gypsy Rose Lee would envy. So, unfortunately, did the ship's MP who descended shortly with the source – a small brown puppy of indeterminate ancestry – which he dropped at my feet and returned to his post.

The pup whimpered, the WAC wept, observers of this dockside drama booed the villain.

At this point, a tardy WAC named Dollie Carpenter who had failed to connect with the last convoy out of Victoria rattled onto the adjoining train siding pumping a hand car in tandem with an obliging railroader who had given her a lift when it looked like she might miss the boat altogether.

The rail birds on deck cheered.

A willing airman smuggled the pup back aboard in his flight jacket.

More cheers.

The eagle-eyed MP brought it back to me.

Boos.

We were just recovering from Dollie's superb performance when a staff car chauffeured by an Australian woman disgorged a young lieutenant, who, after easing his bulging Val-Pak onto the pier, stepped aside to check in with the boarding officer. Without cutting her motor, the driver backed-up – and over – the Val-Pak, consigning to oblivion the entire case of Scotch it contained. For various reasons of health, she kept right on going while the lieutenant fought back his tears.

Boos again – mostly aimed at the disappearing driver by a little knot of outbound WACs who had suffered a major career change partially due to women like her. Having arrived overseas as automotive specialists, they found themselves surplus to SWPA's needs in their field; would be reassigned instead as clerical help.

Swapping tire irons for typewriters proved painful and – to them – a humiliating process, to which end they spent six miserable weeks retraining for desk duties. Although no WACs would be used on the road or in the grease pits of New Guinea as a matter of official policy, those affected always held the local hires personally responsible.

The lieutenant shouldered his soggy Val-Pak, carrying it into the shed behind us for disposal. Instead we emptied scotch and glass shards into a trash bin, hosed out the interior, tucked the puppy inside (now slightly subdued by malt fumes) and the young officer proceeded undetected to reunite the dog with the still-weeping WAC. This time the cheering section had sense enough to shut up.

I learned later the dog reached its New Guinea destination (probably with regret) along with several laying hens two other enterprising WACs smuggled in to revolutionize the island's poultry industry and put fresh meat on the table. Sadly, they did neither, never producing another egg, surviving only as pets.

Ten

North to New Guinea

ETURNING TO Yeronga that day, I found my orders "North" already there. "….trfd in gr to 5205th WAC Det USAFFE…. rptng on arrival to CO for dy with GHQ APO 500…travel by MOCA…personal luggage not to exceed 50 lbs., by command of General MacArthur"

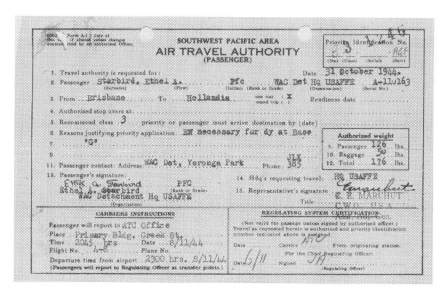

Starbird's travel voucher from Brisbane to Hollandia.

Although Griffith and I would be working at MacArthur's GHQ in Hollandia where it had been located since June, both of us would be assigned to USAFFE, a lesser headquarters: Big Mac still refused to admit WACs to his official family. In fact, during their entire 19 months in SWPA, he publicly acknowledged their presence only twice: in greeting the first six to arrive in Australia and in dispatching the last to leave Manila. But then the ubiquitous Mrs. Roosevelt, the champion of women's rights, ignored us completely in her Pacific wanderings.

The 50-lb baggage limit was bound to bind. It would accommodate a single duffle packed solid as a tackling dummy but provided no space for such New Guinea needments as toilet paper, candles, tooth paste, writing supplies, and those versatile sanitary napkins that doubled as boot polishers, bandages, shirt shields, dust cloths, and packing materials. We had discovered another advantage: layered atop a duffle bag they discouraged luggage inspectors, in this era of easy embarrassment, from digging deeper.

To gain more space, I commissioned the same local artisan who created that aromatic book satchel to construct a regulation size foot locker. Which he did – again a superb job with only one drawback: made of native ironwood, I couldn't lift it even when empty. Finally packed and hauled away by two stalwarts, it was shipped to my next duty station by surface transportation exempt from the 50-lb limit. It arrived five months and three destinations later, its contents a waterlogged mass, its manifest showing stops that it took in Hawaii, Guadalcanal, and just about every other island in the southwest Pacific – the type of circuitous baggage routing commercial airlines took years to perfect.

As a sort of graduation exercise, Lt. Opgrand sent me off to muck out the latrines which a rather indifferent bucket tender had left looking like the Augean stables without the help of Hercules. While hosing away, word came down from the orderly room to report on the double. Which left me no time to pretty up; I double-timed right into the arms of a handsome hometown college friend-turned-flying-officer named Jack Hamilton who gave me a quick bear hug which he probably regretted immediately then took a long look at my single stripe, cruddy boots, rubber gloves, slouch hat, and ill-fitting fatigues. "Hoo, Babe[10]," he said, "bet the class of '38's glad it didn't vote you most likely to succeed."

By way of rebuttal, I mentioned casually that he looked a little pudgier than when last seen.

Since we both knew that his rank couldn't appear publicly with my rank without a lot of written approvals from my commanding officer, we ducked into the day room for a little Auld Lang Syne. In shedding his jacket, Jack also shed his extra poundage, his bulk consisting of a hidden hoard of sandwiches, cheese, pastries, fruit and chocolate bars. "Got fat feet, too," he said, pulling a bottle of scotch from each floppy flight boot. No Brisbane eatery served better.

After Jack returned to his wild blue yondering, I prepared with considerably more care for my next social engagement: the wedding of a young Australian woman with whom I had established friendly foreign relations on our daily commute to town.

Fortunately, mother could solve the gift problem from afar; the bride's fondest wish: a Sears Roebuck catalogue. Oldest of eight children, she and her family occupied one of those neat bungalows on the outskirts of Brisbane into which at least 100 guests sardined for a rousing reception memorable for the quantity of its refreshment and the quality of its fellowship.

With repeated cries of "charge your glasses" we toasted in turn the King, the Queen, Elizabeth the younger, Margaret, and each of several palace Corgis. A thundering rendition of "God Save the King" followed. Then, out of deference to the only Yank present, we downed a separate round of drinks for each member of the family Roosevelt: Franklin, Eleanor, Franklin Jr., Elliott, James, John, Anna and of course Fala. Had they known Anna's kids, Sistie and Buzzie Dahl, were then living in the White House, I never would have made it home. Our national anthem concluded the festivities with almost every Aussie knowing more of the words than I.

---

10   Ethel Starbird was the youngest of the three Starbird siblings, and nicknamed "Babe." As Starbird wrote in 2002: "…I haven't been known by that name since I went in the Army. A few people here are holdovers and though it's a pretty silly name for an 84-yearold, I miss not hearing it."

Opgrand slipped in one last "public relations" chore: addressing a group of teachers-in-training on the U.S. educational system. Probably a logical choice since I had ambled through college in four years and two summer schools. Luckily they were most interested in the non-academic side of campus life, the subject in which I had majored.

To celebrate my now-imminent departure, an Engineer combat team on a brief R&R collected a truckload of us for a picnic in the Tamborine Mountains, some 43 miles northwest of Brisbane. This, my first trip into outback Australia, lacked the smashing impact I had expected: the bowed canvas top of the 6-by in which we traveled permitted only tunnel vision and that only of places already passed. But our destination did not disappoint. There it was – the world when it was new: a magnificent forest of palm and staghorn; of towering trees slick as a fireman's pole rising well over 100 feet above ground before exploding into bird-heavy canopies; of termite mounds taller than tepees and ferns even taller.

Amid this splendid setting the real wartime world intruded: one of the Engineers suffered a wrenching attack of malaria, a consequence not lost on those who were faking taking their Atabrine, mostly for cosmetic reasons.

The most effective anti-malarial drug then available, Atabrine produced one dramatic but harmless side effect: it turned its users a bilious shade of yellow – useful only if a person were trying to "pass" in Peking. WACs on orders began taking the pills at least two weeks before shipping out. But even with a no-nonsense sergeant at the end of the chow line to enforce our one-a-day dosage, evasive action did occur as indicated by an occasional unblemished complexion.

My unnatural color was rising. Now, after four months of computing dollars into pounds, shillings, and pence; of learning that "passing out" had to do with graduation not inebriation; that being "knocked up" in Australia means getting out of bed, not into it, it was time to move on.

Back then, flying had not yet become the mass mover it is today; Mary Poppins had logged more air miles than most of us. Years would pass before we would learn the delights of delayed departures and dining aloft on a packet of peanuts. But military air transport set the pattern for one-class, no-frills service providing no food and, for each passenger, one square foot of seating space in canvas slings strung along both sides of the fuselage. Crushed between two high-calorie corporals, I might have ridden at a modified side-saddle the entire 2,000 miles to Hollandia if a gallant sergeant hadn't yielded his spot atop the lumpy mid-aisle mail sacks – a preferred perch I raced all others to claim in flights to follow.

Shaped like an angry alligator, the island of New Guinea had no trouble dealing with a split personality: British Trust Territory and Paupa administered the eastern half; Dutch New Guinea, now Indonesia's Irian Barat, the western. Hollandia, today's Jayapura, lay just over the international boundary on the Dutch side.

Having retaken most of the eastern half by 1943, the Allies then faced a long and potentially costly struggle to evict the remaining enemy. Rejecting conventional tactics, MacArthur leap-frogged his forces along the north coast, knocking out some strongholds, leaving pockets of resistance to retreat, surrender, or starve.

Hollandia, a coveted prize in this highly effective strategy, not only commanded the superb harbor of Humboldt Bay but also, a few miles inland, three ready-made air strips left by the retreating Japanese. Around these evolved Headquarters Far East Air Forces (FEAF) and its expanding complement of AIRWACS, the pioneering group of enlisted women to arrive in Dutch New Guinea on 31 August '44.

Eleven

Enchanted Evenings in Hollandia, New Guinea

A s I arrived at the coastal settlement, a buck sergeant named Don Something, flashing a great grin and a fullback's physique, scooped up my duffle, tossed it into a waiting jeep, and probably would have opened its door for me had there been one.

"Where to, doll?" he asked.

Doll? Only if we're talking Raggedy Ann not Barbie.

Although most of us had left the States striving with varying success for that sleek June Allyson look, what with bad perms in Australia and none at all in New Guinea, it was difficult to tell these days whether our hair styles derived from indifference or the prop wash from a P-38.

"Let's try for USAFFE," I said.

"Right, doll!"

Oh well... No one had appointed Don official airport greeter; he assumed the role to get the drop on the competition. With the ratio of GIs to WACs running about 100 to 1 (and rising), he felt that being on hand to welcome females of the enlisted persuasion gave him a certain social advantage. He needed all he could get for by evening troops for miles around were trolling around WAC compounds with such tempting date bait as steaks, combat boots, spirit lamps, and soap powder.

Everywhere there were signs that our stay in this latitude would be short. Already the town of Hollandia, with a prewar population of about 200, was pounding together temporary accommodations for a strike force of 200,000 men and their supplies for an all-out effort to retake the Philippines. The huge harbor was fast disappearing beneath a near-solid raft of some 700 war ships and support craft which MacArthur described in his memoirs as "one of the greatest armadas the world has ever known." Sailors going ashore merely walked across parallel decks joined by connecting planks to get there.

For the most part, the 12-mile trip to GHQ followed a gentle, dusty upgrade through bayonet-bladed kunai grass that screened us from all the scenic wonders including the Cyclops Mountains, some more than a mile high, rising on our right. An occasional Afro-headed native, dressed for comfort in a lap-lap and a smile, slipped in and out of the greenery, herding any women in his entourage into complete concealment at the first sound of an approaching vehicle. Word sure gets around.

A few miles out, Don drew up to the probably prototype of today's self-service filling station – a single pump standing unattended beside the road; any driver could tap into it (or the many others like it) whenever and without charge. Don had stopped only to fill his Zippo which when gas-fueled as many of them were for necessity, threw a flame that could cook up a Nip in his cave – or singe the eyebrows of the unwary. My dwindling supply of Chanel No. 5 worked almost as well; at times my lighter smelled more like a debutante than I did.

Soon we were climbing at a steeper pitch – past clusters of quonsets, a civilian-style bungalow built for the MacArthur family (reportedly never occupied), the press camp under canvas, a half-screened PR/Censor building where I would work, and at road's end the USAFFE WAC enclave clumped atop a cliff-sided shelf projecting from the lower elevations of Cyclops' tallest mountain (6,745 feet).

WAC Camp, Hollandia, Dutch New Guinea.

Far below, in a setting Club Med would kill for, lay the unexpected expanse of Lake Sentani with its bordering air fields, expanding facilities of the Far East Air Force conglomerate and, on its mirrored surface, an occasional scratch left by a native canoe or the upscale tribal Cadillac – the *lakitoi* – two salvaged belly tanks rigged like a catamaran.

Not surprisingly, the officers' tents obscured this smashing panorama from all but their own occupants, a situation that inspired a memorable Bill Mauldin cartoon: a captain, admiring a similar scene, comments to his companion: "Beautiful view. Is there one for the enlisted men?" There sure wasn't for enlisted women: with our tent rows facing each other across narrow company streets, we mostly admired each other.

Although USAFFE WACs lived under conditions similar to those elsewhere in the theater, our altitude was admittedly more agreeable than most. Located some three degrees off the Equator we shared with those at sea level daytime temperatures that often reached 100 degrees F or more, but where we cooled off a little a night, few of them did. Otherwise ours was a typical SWPA WAC installation.

More for privacy than protection, bolts of burlap, stretched over five strands of fence wire, enclosed the property on three sides while the cliff face in front of the officers' line took care of the rest. Whether these precautions were designed to keep intruders out or residents in remains debatable.

Social life at every WAC encampment proceeded under similar semi-stalag conditions. Those not working ten to twelve hour shifts, which many were, could leave the area between 1800 and 2200 with an approved escort providing he carried a weapon, brought transportation, and invited along at least one other couple as sort of a "safety in numbers" ploy. To comply with these requirements one GI rolled up in a DUKW armed with a 30 mm cannon and urged half the camp to come aboard.

Destination would be determined by a coin-toss. There were only two possibilities: the movies showing just about everywhere every night or the less frequent unit party if your date happened to be on the guest list. Whatever the choice, one rule prevailed: absolutely no stops or detours along the way. An entire evening could be spent playing hide-and-seek with the MPs sent out to enforce it.

No one believed these proscriptions would promote celibacy but, wild rumors to the contrary, illegitimate pregnancies – elective or accidental – rarely disrupted SWPA life. Of our 5,500 WACs, only 111 returned home pregnant and half of them were already married. Even in those far less permissive days, the rate was far higher among US civilians.

Oddly, routine gyno exams so annoyingly frequent stateside completely disappeared in this coed situation that should encourage them. Thus, one mother-to-be escaped detection for nine months; was required to birth her babe in Hollandia where scores of GI pretend parents – male and female – helped handcraft a suitable layette: lahala-woven bassinet padded with parachute cloth, swaddling clothes of the same material, booties and sweaters of fly-in wool from Australia which even the Marines helped knit on needles they painstakingly whittled from stems of bamboo. One group even tucked a $500 savings bond under the blanket cut from someone's nightgown. "After all," reasoned one of the project's participants, "whoever the father is, it's gotta be one of us. Right?" Right!

Earlier occupants of our aerie had left behind several rows of cement tent floors, privy-type latrines with oil-barrel seats like the one that blew away one soldier's family ties; also a combination orderly-supply room, mess hall, and the frame of a future recreation building. Enlisted men from all services, ever the sultans of scrounge, raised our tents and spirits, providing many of the basics that made life under canvas almost home-like – at least to those used to sharing a room with five sisters.

Salvage parachutes in decorator colors – red, blue, yellow, green – floated as false ceilings from the overhead tent vents; bolts of burlap, ruffled and fringed, feminized packing box dressers and nail keg stools (when fabric supplies ran low more were obtained by snipping away at the back side of our stockade.) Empty wire spools served well as night stands, #16 cans as trash containers. With Christmas fast approaching, we encouraged offerings of rope and wire to transform broom handles into Yule trees, can tops into cut ornaments. Sun seekers began appearing in swim suits fashioned from two GI towels and a handful of boot laces.

In this company, Martha Stewart wouldn't make corporal.

Muggier climes at lower levels offered more fertile soil, promoting a lively trade in garden seeds. Horticultural efforts produced some amazing results – in size if not in substance. Tendrils from one planting threatened to swallow several tents; legumes shooting skyward like Jack's beanstalk failed to bear a single pod; carrots exploded into lush tops, no bottoms.

Appetites anticipating an orgy of fresh vegetables were forced to settle for more of the usual – canned or dehydrated. (When one young woman entered the mess hall proudly brandishing an Aussie-grown cucumber of impressive proportions, fellow diners whittled it to her thumb joint before she could sit down.) Inevitably, foodstuffs raised below ground – carrots, beets, potatoes, turnips – appeared cut into cubes, reinforcing my dislike for anything to do with square roots and my conviction that Gerber held the canning contract.

Two other mainstays of SWPA existence deserve at least passing attention: the triple-spouted Lyster bag from which all drinking water flowed and New Guinea's very special blend of coffee.

The first always sat out in full sun, its contents burbling at slightly below boil, its taste enhanced by enough chlorine to purify a public swimming pool. Starting with the same water, flavored more with chicory than the bean, diluted if at all with tinny-tasting canned milk, Guinea blend coffee had all the appeal of paint remover. Then too, by the time the rolled metal rim on the canteen cup cooled enough <u>not</u> to cauterize on contact, its contents had already begun to congeal.

Although experiments with animal husbandry had failed, private menageries flourished. One camp shared its limited space and rations with four dogs, a pigmy pig on a lunge line, three monkeys of unattractive habits, a goat, and several exotic birds some GI Jungle Jims had collected in the highlands.

When it came to sources of supply, the enlisted man was, undisputedly, the most inventive and inexhaustible. Among our more prized acquisitions: a mobile refrigerator slightly smaller than a house trailer that mysteriously appeared attached to our mess hall one misty morning, donor unknown. Sought for months as a "most wanted" by the MP detachment from whom it was detached, it hummed along happily at our place until some fink revealed its whereabouts. So much for police work.

Not to be outdone, a Seabee unit down the hill – both men and machines – rolled through our gates one dawn and within two days, its warriors, on rest leave, had completed a rec hall large enough to house a Goodyear blimp, equipped it with a dance floor, band stand, bamboo tables and chairs, even coconut shell ashtrays and a screened-in telephone booth through which contact with the outside world seldom materialized. When they finally ran out of "liberated" lumber, they hired a native crew to fill in the empty spaces with an attractive palm-frond lattice work known as lahala. Naturally, those "can do" guys who did so much for us were our first guests.

Within the USAFFE compound, my property rights consisted of a small corner of a six person tent already so stuffed with homemade improvements it resembled a back country rummage sale. Dumping my duffle and a bundle of sticks the supply sergeant assured me would convert into a cot; I thumbed a ride down the hill to see how my new boss was faring without me.

Extremely well, it seems. Griffith had, in the past three weeks, worked wonders with the press corps, convincing skeptics among them to focus on the plus side of the WAC presence, less on the minus side, real or imaginary. Her candor, humor, and killer game of cribbage had won – beside their money – the cooperation and respect of many of the day's top by-liners. Some even named her surrogate kin to decide what among their belongings would be shipped home if their owners couldn't make it. (About this time, the Press Corps lost three of its number in a single air raid on Tacloban.)

My job: cranking out home town releases, combing the countryside for feature material of possible press pool interest or Washington rewrite, and keeping the cribbage board dusted. Our work space, carved from the back end of a cavernous building otherwise occupied by SWPA public relations and military censors left room for improvement: it contained Griffith's lieutenant-level field desk and canvas chair and, for me, a camp stool, a packing-box table to type on, an aging Underwood, 3-drawer file (the bottom one was missing), one 40-watt bulb, and a wire waste basket. Oh, yes, and an extremely temperamental telephone which even when working did so erratically.

Calls, no matter over how short a distance were relayed through numerous exchanges before reaching their destination (if ever) and male operators did nothing to speed the process once they heard the unfamiliar voice of a woman winging down the wire.

"Hello. This is Glider."

"Glider, this is Bandaid. I'm trying to get Gunsmoke."

"Hey, honey, you must be one of those WACs."

"I am. Now will you put me through to Gunsmoke?"

"Where you from in the States, WAC?"

"Vermont. So let's get on with the nation's business."

"Say, I had an uncle in Vermont. Brattleboro. You doing anything Saturday night?"

"Look, soldier, my boss is not amused by this delay. She'd like your name, rank, and serial number."

Ethel Starbird, Hollandia, Dutch New Guinea
(Photo Attributed to Frank"Frankie"Filan)

"Okay! Okay! Gunsmoke you say? I'll have to patch you through Iodine, Glider, and Rocket. If there's a tie up anywhere along the line, you'll be rerouted through Wig-Wag, Jump Zone and probably Bivouac. I take it that's a no for Saturday. Well, here goes, tighten your seatbelt, enjoy your trip."

Multiply that by the total of relay operators and the time in transit for a single call could take hours. About as long as it takes today to get someone to explain your phone bill.

In preparing our work place, the contractor overlooked one small detail: a latrine of the feminine gender, the nearest being our WAC enclave a mile or so away to which we were jeeped noon and night, never in-between. Our office-mates – all male – partially solved the problem: they would, on call, run interference for us to the men's facility in the press camp next door. Given the acoustics and barn-like proportions of our shared space, the only way to announce our need was bellow; whoever felt cooperative at that moment, answered at equal volume. The encounter was not a clandestine one. I may be the only PFC in history to be escorted to the bathroom by a bird colonel of the opposite sex.

Sometimes, the response was doubtful. Hearing a combat zone would soon be re-designated as secure, the officers would wangle temporary duty there thus acquiring in perfect safety a battle star to accessorize their SWPA service ribbon and another five points toward early discharge at war's end.

A second Seebee outfit came to our rescue. Billeted on a bluff overlooking our office, a delegation appeared at our door one afternoon to propose a trade: they'd provide me with lunch every day for a few spirited games of ping pong and my noon-time presence. Griffith, a Hoosier horse trader at heart, upped the ante: a two-holer in our back yard or I couldn't come out and play. A done deal. They built one in two hours, including a set of steps down the bluff and a dressing table swathed in frilled burlap. The crescent moon carved into its door took a little longer.

The SWPA WACs' most acute problem: clothing suitable for tropic wear. One Oro Bay contingent arrived with nothing but Artic gear, a weird situation since no wartime WACs ever drew duty much farther north than Maine. Those two pairs of mild-weather fatigues issued in Oglethorpe proved adequate for shipboard, unnecessary for Australia, and totally inappropriate for New Guinea where their texture and weight caused skin problems and their baggy design did little to repel those who held air supremacy in these parts – mosquitoes.

Although Hobby cringed at the thought of her troops in trousers, conditions in SWPA offered no alternative. A trip to our area would have confirmed her worst fears: native trash collectors, confused by our costumes, covered all bases by calling us "boy-girl."

We finally received the stateside answer for the climate and circumstances: a voluminous two-piece ensemble with knee-nuzzling crotch and thigh-high pockets which, if used, would pad us where no woman needed it. Only those natives sweltering proudly through their clean-up chores in our cast-off winter issue loved them. But then, they admired the Hobby hat so much they often wore as many as three stacked atop their beehive hairdos.

Rejecting these Pentagon-inspired imports as an insult to our fashion sense, we returned to a more reliable shopping source – male order.

As my fatigues frayed, so, too, did my interest in Don; his generous dimensions precluded my annexing any of his wardrobe. But in Frankie Filan I had found a near perfect match – 32R. An Associated Press photographer with a half-dozen assault landings under his 30 inch belt (easily notched to fit me) he had won a Pulitzer[11] for his gritty coverage of the Tarawa operation. All that leaping on and off beaches under fire kept him thin, slim, and – thankfully – close to my measurements.

No one could possibly mis-judge our relationship: at that time and place, a serious liaison was suspected only if a WAC kept company with a fellow whose clothes she could not wear.

To complete our wardrobe, it was sometimes necessary to shop all the services. Which is how I came to be wearing, all at the same time, a Navy overseas cap, Marine shirt, Seabee dungarees, Air Corps jacket, and jungle boots courtesy of the Japanese Imperial Army. The effect was so stunning Frankie insisted on photographing

---

11   Frank "Frankie" Filan won a Pulitzer Prize while working for the Associated Press in 1944 for a picture of a blasted Japanese bunker on Tarawa titled "Tarawa Island."

me for the family album in every junkyard of downed Zeros and Bettys for miles around. Given the number of wrecked planes in these pictures, my parents wondered how come the war was taking so long.

Ethel Starbird, Hollandia, Dutch New Guinea.
(Photo attributed to Frank "Frankie" Filan)

Ethel Starbird, Hollandia, Dutch New Guinea.
(Photo attributed to Frank"Frankie"Filan)

All this metal scrap fueled a profitable cottage industry for the typewriter repair T-5, whose turnaround time for an ailing Royal or Remington suddenly stretched into weeks while he would, overnight and for $20, fashion a sweat-proof watch band from a snippet of plane wing; for $20 more he'd emboss it with genuine Japanese characters pried from an instrument panel. Judging from the planes' riddled condition, he returned home with his retirement already paid for.

Entrepreneurs emerged in other unlikely places. The demand for Christmas photos from the battlefront rocketed anyone with a camera (forbidden all troops for security reasons) to the top of the popularity poll. One Signal Corps WAC, no rose to begin with, quickly filled her purse and her dance card when word circulated that she had access to cameras, film, and a dark room. Her charge for a wallet-size snap – a month's ration of either beer or cigarettes or $20 in cash. This Karsh-under-canvas would, for another $10, provide warlike props to impress the home folks with the dangers of our mission, a practice frowned on by the censors. One supply-type WAC was busted for trying to smuggle out a photo of herself posed with Patton-like ferocity wearing a 45 Colt automatic pistol on each hip. Back then, the only arms WACs were permitted to carry were their own.

Perhaps the most successful of these upfront tycoons was a buck sergeant named Belden whose extra-curricular activities revealed themselves when I pulled Charge of Quarters (CQ) one evening. Duty at that time of day consisted mainly of summoning those with dates on the PA system as their escorts arrived. Those who opted to stay on campus were confined to the rec hall where every move was monitored by an attentive and often opinionated audience. That scene did not appeal to Belden.

She responded to an early call but from the orderly room I didn't notice if she went to the rec hall or out the front gate. A half-hour later, another GI cleared the guard and asked for Belden. "Sorry, fella," I said, "there must be some mistake. She's already engaged for the evening."

"Aw, c'mon, WAC. She may be disengaged by now. Giver her a yell anyway, will ya?"

Mostly to get him out of the office, I obliged. Almost immediately here came Belden tripping up from the tent rows to wander off into the fast-descending darkness with caller number two. And so it went in something over half-hour intervals until lock-up time at ten.

Being curious about her trysting place, I retraced her route as I remembered it the next morning. Well beaten, it led over a knoll beyond public view but still within the compound and into an abandoned Japanese machine gun emplacement cozily fitted with a mattress from some mysterious source and a protective tarp. Here Belden – best described here as user friendly – was out-earning MacArthur less than 100 yards from our CO's office.

Some killjoy later blew the whistle on her, but the brass, after much huddling and muddling, could find no rule in the *Army Regulations* or *Articles of War* that quite fit this situation. At the time those bibles of military behavior had yet to describe her exact crime: she hadn't left the reservation without permission, fraternized by the Army definition, nor, being unwed herself and lacking interest in the marital status of her clients, could she be accused of adultery in the strict sense. So, after pondering the case for several days, the CO decided to ship Belden off to a Postal unit at Oro Bay where mail-handling was an approved activity. (At which, incidentally, the WACs overseas excelled - having the patience and persistence in tracking troops on the move and getting mail to them with a minimum time in transit.)

I really hated to see Belden leave. We pulled KP the same days and, both being long limbed, usually ended up sharing pots, pans – and an occasional confidence. But as close as we came on these swab jobs, she never confided how she laundered her considerable fortune to get it home. It must have been doubly difficult since, for some obscure reason, all SWPA military were paid in coin of the realm – Dutch guilders – although the only place they could be spent was in a PX or ship's store which in our case was the size of a broom closet – or to pay the supply sergeant for our monthly ration of 3 cartons of cigarettes or 1 12-bottle case of beer. The most logical way to export her earnings: to enlist an obliging airman to fly her loot to Australia, exchange it there for US dollars, then send the converted currency through local post office or bank. Until someone blew her cover, she was often in a position to return the favor.

What with clock-around guards and stockade-like security, we thought little if any about uninvited visitors. But with all that pulchritude perched within sight of a dozen all-male camp sites, it was probably inevitable that one day some sly fox would sneak into our hen yard.

The night was right: flood lights were dimmed, bed check long over, the entire area lay in deep shadow and even deeper slumber. A corporal, coverless in the heat in the tent across the way, awoke with her leg in an unauthorized grip whose owner murmured intimate suggestions through the mosquito bar. Her screams discouraged further explorations and, at the same time, roused every recumbent WAC within earshot.

"It's a man!" bellowed the corporal. "Get the bastard!"

The place exploded; an aardvark in an anthill couldn't have done it better. Women in various stages of undress spilled out of every tent, brandishing whatever weapon came to hand – mess kits, beer bottles, steel helmets, even an occasional native spear acquired in a Hobby hat swap. Chances of identifying the intruder in this melee became immediately impossible; everyone – except maybe those wearing curlers – was considered fair game.

"I've got him," yelped one warrior, whanging out with a mess kit.

"The hell you have. It's me – Dottie."

"Take that!" whooped a roller-derby type as she flattened a hazy figure in the pathway. Who proved to be the company clerk.

A helmeted camper launched herself like an unguided missile into the fray, taking out the mess sergeant. I collapsed under a tackle worthy of the NFL.

Uprooting guy ropes in their frenzy, the defenders managed to bring down at least one tent before the skirmish ended. Fortunately, injuries from friendly fire were few but, unfortunately, the culprit made a clean getaway. Probably through the snipped-out portions of burlap along the back fence. After that, flood lights remained on high beam all night and visitors to the latrine went armed, accompanied, or both.

Only one other trespasser dropped in during my stay – and in full daylight, at that. Sneaking into the farthest latrine abutting the back fence, he closed the door, settled onto the oil-drum commode and crossed his legs to await his prey in relative comfort. Enter left:

an off-duty WAC to do her laundry in one of the shallow troughs provided for this purpose. Sensing something amiss she sidled out, summoned aid, and together they caught the interloper with his pants still in place.

"Yeah, but how'd you know it wasn't one of us in there?" someone asked.

"Showing only one leg in a size 13 boot? Y'gotta be kidding. Sit-down women floor both feet. Check it out!" answered our queen-for-a-day. Genuflecting before the abbreviated doors of closed cubicles became a common rite.

Most visitors to our Shangri La arrived by invitation, usually whisking their dates off to one of the two approved forms of off-campus entertainment. The more intimate jeep parties cruised until they found and outdoor movie with parking space somewhere this side of Kamchatka. Distance didn't make much difference anyway. The film was bound to break just as the action was heating up which led to a similar situation in the jeep seats.

Unit parties, the only other option for a night out in New Guinea, bore a certain resemblance to a cattle roundup. Packed into that Far East limo – the 6-by truck – we were chuted earthward at the market place without hurry so those awaiting could consider our relative merits, each hoping no doubt to cut a likely heifer from the herd. The 3 hours of Lindy Hopping that followed in "his" and "her" combat boots left virtually no shin unscarred. But its survivors certainly reinforced Darwin's theory of natural selection.

Naturally, sustaining all this energy required a certain amount of medical attention – namely a liberal supply of 90 proof hospital alcohol flavored but slightly with a dash of canned fruit juice – pineapple, grapefruit, whatever. For a real touch of elegance, one host group served this GI gin in honest-to-God tumblers cleverly contrived by filling empty beer bottles to just below the neck with engine oil, inserting a hot poker which broke the glass cleanly at that level, then sanding the rims to Anchor-Hocking smoothness. The immediate effect was something like kissing your crank case – but after a few swallows, the taste of petroleum faded – so, too, did a certain number of revelers.

Twelve

I Won't Be Home For Christmas

WITH CHRISTMAS waiting in the wings, the Press camp – where rank or lack thereof never mattered – opened the holiday season with a real rouser. To which an uninvited guest contributed hugely.

Early in the festivities, for which Griffith and I had assembled the comeliest WACs available – officer or enlisted – I wandered outside to admire one of New Guinea's trademark Technicolor sunsets which, though brief, suggested Jackson Pollock had kicked over his paint cans behind a drift of deckled-edged clouds.

A dusty jeep joined me, disgorging a wiry little fellow and six matched, unscratched, cowhide suitcases – perfect for the Plaza but definitely mold bait for our part of the Pacific. Easy to guess he was neither military nor newsman – he wore spotless sun tans with pant creases so sharp they looked stropped.

"Pardon me, ma'm," he said in a rather gravelly voice, "I seem to be lost. You haven't seen this is the Army around here anywhere, have you?"

"As a matter of fact, that's all I've seen anywhere for the last 18 months."

"No, no. I'm talking about the USO troupe that's out here playing the jungle circuit with the show "This Is The Army." I'm meant to be joining them."

"Haven't heard of them reaching this end of the island. You play one of the parts?"

"Well, sort of." He stuck out his hand. "Name's Irving Berlin."

Stranded with us for several days while he tracked down his misplaced road company, Mr. Berlin not only brightened the Press camp revels that evening, he also traveled about the immediate area entertaining, among others, our WAC detachment with a 2-hour medley of Berlin originals. I adored the man; his was the only singing voice in SWPA worse than mine.

Except for Berlin and a turkey dinner with all the fixings, Christmas day was much like any other. We worked a regular shift but in the late afternoon an in-house Santa in borrowed combat boots, Kotex beard, and a similarly trimmed costume fashioned from a bright red ammo chute ho-hoed through the area distributing fruit, candy, and nuts from a barracks bag.

My parents had chosen well; their package contained such Guinea usables as calcium pills, T-shirts, Webster's Collegiate Dictionary, and a Boy Scout knife with built-in bottle opener. The town of Jericho sent a sewing kit, my sister a rare pint of Johnny Walker cushioned inside a loaf of bread, one of the safer ways to ship breakables in those days. The gurgle must have given the game away: the box arrived as neatly wrapped as when shipped, the loaf's two halves firmly stuck together, no crumb misplaced. But the spirits had been spirited away in transit.

Although Postal clerks worked mightily to keep mail moving, excessive Christmas traffic and tracing troop whereabouts slowed, often stalled, the delivery system. Packages accumulated at improvised depots, spilling from under inadequate tarps, being soaked by daily downpours. Wrappings dissolved, addresses washed away.

Statesiders had been cautioned to include a duplicate address inside all packages. Some didn't. So, naturally, mail undeliverable and un-returnable became something of a problem. Which those attending its storage and disposal solved quite handily: in the great American tradition, they became Yankee traders, emerging from the Santa season wearing more watches than a Tangier street peddler, offering a ready supply of fountain pens, safety razors, flashlights and toenail clippers.

Not all parents were as practical as mine. One of my tent-mates named Dawson failed to inform her family of the rather circumscribed circumstances under which we lived: her mother sent along one of those cute little zippered bags which, when stuffed with a pair of pajamas, shaped up into a loveable puppy throw pillow for the bed.

What pajamas? A throw pillow?

A breakdown of communication also led to some unfortunate food choices. Back-home folks shaved their already minimal meal allowance, saving ration stamps for something special for the troops. I don't know at what sacrifice my mother accumulated enough to include ten cans of Vienna Sausage; I was amazed there were that many left on earth after being served them at every mess hall meal since we arrived in Australia. Even natives scavenging for leftovers shunned them.

Most veterans emerge from service with a few food phobias. My father, back from World War I, never ate canned peaches again. For me, I will forever forego Vienna Sausage and apple butter. No matter how fast or slow a chow line moved; no matter what a mess kit already contained – corn flakes, mashed potatoes, coleslaw, custard – the final server buried the whole mess beneath a tsunami of apple butter.

Any attempt to duck out of line to escape this culinary catastrophe was thwarted by the non-com monitoring our Atabrine intake.

While a WAC bunking across from me begged for a bathtub in an open letter to Santa penned to her tent fly, faithful friend Frankie actually found one for me – a galvanized beauty 12 inches deep, 22 inches in diameter – the kind used well into the 20th century for laundry and forever at our backwoods camp in Maine for Saturday night baths.

I had wearied of hanging chimp-like from a pull chain – the only way our New Guinea showers worked – while trying to effectively scour everything with only one hand. I yearned to sit down, even pretzel-fashion, for the first time in my military career and contemplate the bottoms of my feet. Having taken a beating for much of that time, they deserved the attention.

It never happened. The tub could only be filled by standing in it directly beneath the shower and yanking, getting thoroughly drenched while accumulating very little water. I abandoned the entire project and with it all hope of adding to my earnings with rentals – or ever getting my feet clean.

Hauling the tub into an unused corner of our campus, I prepared to go into the laundry business. After months of scouring our clothes in cold water and little if any soap, they were so grime laden they crackled when we walked. After filling the tub a helmetful at a time, scrounging fuel from the kitchen crate dump and setting it aflame, I dumped in some of my own clothes for a trail run and wandered off to do other chores assuming boiling water would do my work. It did, all right: the tub boiled dry, burning my britches and just about everything else I owned behind me. So ended my hopes of becoming a battlefront tycoon.

However, extra cash was available from yet another source: reselling monthly rations of cigarettes and beer to those with a greater craving. Three cartons of cigarettes bought at one dollar each went easily at twenty dollars apiece; the 24-bottle case of beer drew lively bids of up to fifty dollars. In civilian circles, they branded this type of transaction black marketing; we liked to think of it as doing a good buddy a favor.

Actually, parting with a beer ration wasn't that much of a sacrifice. Constantly churned in transit and heated to toddy temperature by the South Pacific sun, an opened bottle would usually geyser half its content skyward before a mouth could stopper its flow.

Living this close to the Equator, days began and ended with surprising speed; we saw no lingering dawns and dusks as in the temperate zone – dark came and went in one helluva hurry. Those out and about on our treeless tract just before daybreak rose early to welcome home our night fighters as they screamed past at eye-level and close in - waggling their wings and lifting their thumbs in a cheery salute. By answer we pumped our fists aloft until they dissolved into the anthill of aircraft in the valley below. We were in love with every one of them.

To us this seemed quite enough activity before breakfast and a truck trip down hill to work. But someone thought otherwise.

Certainly the unused drill field could be put to more soldierly purpose than as a grandstand for this early a.m. air show.

By now it was generally conceded that little if anything could be done to improve our personal appearance. Somehow, the beautician promised for each WAC detachment got folded into some more critical MOS and hair once "neat and off the collar" was chopped with any dull instrument or none at all. The rare and innovative home permanents then to reach our shores produced coiffures strikingly similar to those of the native trash collectors with the ammonia aroma of a newly-cleaned public toilet.

After too little consideration, someone decided our sagging posture and shuffling gait needed serious attention. So instead of rising just before six we would henceforth fall out at 5:15 a.m. for an organized walk-about the Army way.

When the canned bugle notes sounded, Cyclops still slept behind a curtain of clouds, the camp lying in such dense darkness the entire Japanese army could have passed through undetected. For the next half-hour we stumbled around to the disembodied chant of M/Sgt Willie Carr who, among other talents, was the hottest honky tonk piano player this side of Honolulu's Hotel Street.

We couldn't see where we were going – and neither could Willie. So with each flanking movement, some fell out of formation and back into bed; by the time Willie barked "dismissed" few had hung around to hear her.

By week's end the reveille turn-out was becoming too thin to remain convincing. So each tent selected one representative to answer roll call for the rest and to pound ground loud enough to sound like six. The only one to receive no benefit from this charade was the formidable Willie who, convinced that when company officers didn't have enough to do they gave sergeants more, called a halt to all this nonsense while those who devised it never even noticed.

Thirteen

North, On the Road to Victory

OBVIOUSLY, WE would not shape up before we shipped out – yet again. Which should be soon now - although the closer we came to combat the less we knew about the war's progress. Those with access to dispatches kept us updated on recent conquests, dropping intriguing names like Ulithi, Palau, Morotai, Numfoor, and Anguam – but no one knew for sure where any of them were. Even if they had, who could track the action – the front was all over the place. By now, the Allies were racing well ahead of the headlines that reached us days, even weeks, late through our only new sources – *Midpacifican*, a sparce service paper published in Honolulu, and occasional copy of *Stars and Stripes*, and pony editions of *Time*.

So when those stationed at Hollandia-by-the-Sea awoke on October 14 to an empty harbor, it could only be assumed that the invasion of the Philippines had begun, whereabouts unknown. Within the week, we learned the Allied forces had landed on Leyte, 1,300 miles to the northwest of us but only 295 air miles south of Manila. From this position in mid-archipelago, the attack could move in either direction – south to Mindinao, north to Luzon. Mac was back!

Spiffy in starched suntans, he waded ashore on October 20 just four hours behind the first assault wave, leading some to marvel that he walked through water, not on it. (With considerably more chutzpah, George Patton made a similar splash when he reached the Rhine; with a zip and a flip he added to its flow in an action photo still treasured by anyone lucky enough to own a copy.)

In rallying the Filipino people to keep up the good fight, MacArthur, in his celebrated "I have returned" proclamation neglected to mention a few others who helped – 257,766 ground troops, hundreds of magnificent men in their flying machines, much of the 3rd Fleet, and almost all of the 7th. For getting him there and guaranteeing his foothold, we paid a high price: 3,500 killed, 12,000 wounded.

Although the Battle of Leyte Gulf preceding MacArthur's arrival decimated Japan's dwindling air and sea power and marked a major turning point in the Pacific war, the enemy entrenched on the island fought bitterly until Ormoc fell on December 11, 1944. Almost a month earlier, and only five weeks after the initial landing, the first WACs – Griffith among them – took off to Tacloban, the provincial capital. Her departing words: "Remember, Starbird, they also serve who only sit and wait."

The waiting I accepted, although not graciously, but the sitting part presented something of a problem. For, as soon as Griffith left, so, too, did our office furnishings – through a form of Army procurement best remembered as moonlight requisitioning. The tables vanished first, then the chairs, and finally our only light bulb. Just as I learned to squat on a sunbeam to do my typing, the typewriter disappeared.

Although our midnight cowboy showed no interest in the files, I thought it best to ship them along to Griffith should she decide to write her memoirs. As it turned out, she didn't want them either. Which is just as well – they never arrived and may even now be in the burial ground of lost luggage – Hong Kong.

Whoever the pillager was, he displayed a certain bravura: a sprig of wild orchids awaited me in a battered canteen cup after each nocturnal raid.

Without a typewriter, my output stuttered to a stop: it seemed absurd to multi-copy releases in a handwriting few could decipher. So I filled some idle hours participating in the latest camp craze.

Long before the beat-up Volks bus crowd began tie-dying everything but the commune-cat, their mothers-to-be, stationed "somewhere in the South Pacific" were dipping knotted T-shirts into the only coloring compound available – dissolved Atabrine tablets filched from the mess hall. With only helmets to soak them in and no hot water to set the dye, the swirls, pinwheels, and sunburst that appeared weren't exactly Picasso but they did leave indelible imprints of the same jaundiced yellow our bodies now bore from Atabrine absorption (which total abstinence would fade in about three months.) While the ultra chic may tint their dogs, hair, and motor cars to create an ensemble, we may be the only ones ever to dye our shirts to match our skin.

Although surrounded by some pretty spectacular scenery, our immediate environs remained a monotonous, monochromatic brown – from the dust underfoot to darker tones cast by weathered canvas overhead. Small wonder we sometimes went to extremes to put a little color in our lives. Which probably wouldn't have been possible without the humble T-shirt which World War II transformed into a permanent part of unisex apparel. Since then its popularity has further transformed it into a body billboard for every place, project, and product on the face of the globe. But to us, it was underwear, nightshirt, occasionally a swim top and, in extremis, a cleaning cloth of great versatility.

My favorite fashion designer will ever remain *Fruit of the Loom.*

About the time I ran out of T-shirts, one of the correspondents ran through the office flogging a Hermes, a compact, light-weight typewriter easily carried in a duffle or musette bag. About the size of today's laptop. His price: $65, more than my month's pay but raisable by pledging my rations in advance. Although I accepted going to war as my patriotic duty, I sure hadn't expected to pay for the privilege.

A few days later, Henry McLemore, a syndicated columnist from Atlanta turned soldier-journalist, dropped by to propose and even swap: his standard portable Remington for my less cumbersome Hermes which I disliked anyway. After prying another $10 out of him, we had a deal.

While Henry was somewhere up the line and safely out of reach, I discovered a little ID plate riveted to the underside of the Remington reading: "Property of the United States Government."

Naturally I did the only reasonable thing under the circumstances: I pried off the identification and after dragging the machine around for eight more years, sold it in Tokyo for $85. Not without misgivings though: the battered case emblazoned with "GHQ, APO 500, San Fran" made me look rather professional I thought (though Maggie Higgins might disagree) and led to many a shared drink with fellow travelers who actually were.

A sketch of life at GHQ by Starbird, sent home to her family.

Griffith sent word that she wearied of trying to scrounge supplies; officers never were much good at the larceny thing (except for liberating gold bullion and art masterpieces.) I was ordered to proceed without delay to join her.

So the week after Christmas again found me queued up to board a DC-3, those wonderful work horses of WWII. A trio of GIs, assembled to watch the WACS sway their way up a cargo net and into the plane's belly, assured me the scenery was worth the wait.

"Where ya headed, WAC?" one asked.

"Leyte." I said, since the information was no longer classified.

"Isn't there still a lot of action up there?"

"A little, I guess. Mop up. So what outfit you guys with?"

"Combat engineers. Remember us? We're the fellows you freed to fight. So who gets the call to combat. You go, we stay. When it comes to screw-ups, no one can top the US Army."

Tacloban, as seen from the back end of a truck, would not have excited their envy. The covering tarp not only restricted the view which wasn't much any time; it sagged beneath a deluge that would have swamped Noah. The Allies' push into Leyte coincided with the start of the rainy season on an island usually awash with some 100 inches a year.

Pureed by massive military traffic, byways became endless troughs of mud the color and consistency of wet cement, concealing craters capable of ingesting whole jeeps, regurgitating only their riders.

Torrential downpours, often of typhoon ferocity, slowed the Allied advance; costly skirmishes in the mountains sent casualty numbers soaring. Stuffed to the seams with invasion forces, Tacloban suffered a severe housing shortage with hospital units often operating within bomb-ravaged churches; in one a few miles to the south, screen actor Lew Ayres lived out his Dr. Kildare role – as a combat medic. Those who worshipped here did so among the sick and wounded.

Tents, roped together for stability, crowded so tightly onto their sites rain sluicing down one roof funneled through the rolled up sides of its neighbor. And out in the craft-clogged harbor, the doughty old SS Mactan rode at anchor with an unusual cargo of 70 WACs as well as the top staff and person of Maj. Gen. James E. Frink, head honcho of the entire SWPA Services of Supply.

Frink, one of our most ardent supporters (along with Col. Ginsburgh) insisted that for uninterrupted efficiency the most essential of the many WACs assigned to his headquarters move up to Leyte with the first support echelons. With no space available ashore, he offered to share his own accommodations – the SS Mactan – in what may remain the Army's most successful experiment in early gender integration.

Both ship and women had already logged an impressive amount of sea duty. The former, of German origin, fell into US hands during World War I, plied peacefully between Luzon and Mindinao until the start of WWII when it evacuated some 400 wounded Americans from the Philippines to Australia, eventually steaming into Hollandia harbor to become Frink's floating HQ both there and in Leyte.

Its resident WACs, now seasoned sailors, had ridden the sea lanes from San Francisco to Australia to New Guinea to the Philippines (with land-based billets in between) only to remain afloat in Leyte, bunking down aboard the Mactan for an indefinite stay. Their accommodations, though snug, offered advantages denied those ashore: sundeck privileges, porthole laundry service, dry sleeping space, and ship-side shopping from bum boats swarming around each evening as ants at a picnic to peddle for extortionist prices such merchandise as shower clogs made from old tires ($10 US), sculptured coconut husks ($10 US), pina cloth ($25 US a yard), the detritus left by the retreating Japanese ($$$ US.)

Although several other WACs rode the same plane to Tacloban with me, they disappeared on landing into the mudscape while I hitched a ride with a mail clerk to upscale lodgings in a two-story mission school already occupied by some thirty earlier arrivals. Our squad room covered the entire top floor while classes for kids we never saw continued in a similar space below. A chapel still operated at one end of our barracks area; at the other end WAC officers (including Griffith) now billeted where resident nuns once were, so naturally instructions issuing from that quarter became known as "holy orders."

Stretched full-length across the back of the main building, a double porch with connecting stairways overlooked a latrine area of now familiar design, a floating board walk, a fallout shelter so awash with critters and crud it would take another raid on Dresden to force anyone into it, and a cluster of pyramidal tents doubling as a station hospital.

Despite near-constant rains – 34 inches fell during 40 days of the Leyte campaign – our personal water supply remained woefully inadequate. Gravity-fed from a rooftop tank sieved by

WAC Billet (upstairs at a Catholic school), Tacloban, Leyte, Philippine Islands.

shrapnel, whatever accumulated above the half-way mark exited at once. This permitted only one shower every 24 hours, sufficient perhaps under normal conditions but far from it with daily temperatures rising above 100 degrees and humidity shooting off the charts.

Fortunately, laundry no longer drained our water rations; local ladies now bundled it off to some rocky riverbed to pummel it squeaky clean in exchange for most of our monthly salary. In the process, they introduced into whatever they washed a lingering essence of scorched rice starch, the charcoal that fired native flat irons, a musky smell of mildew, and subtle reminders of whatever floated downstream. I regretted squandering all of my Chanel No. 5 to light my Luckies.

Allocated about 24 square feet of squad room, I dropped my duffle, set up my strip-of-canvas cot and its protective mosquito bar on which perky little geckos began immediately to trampoline. Cute? To a point. However, failure to keep the net tucked tight at all times encouraged these canny, clammy masters of disguise, their family, and their friends, to move in down below.

Personal space, never lavish, seemed to shrink as we moved

north. Carry-out laundry service solved part of the problem: with such a scanty wardrobe, we usually kept half on our back, half in the wash at all times. Bare essentials – foot and tooth powder; tooth, nail and hair brushes, calcium pills; my father's World War I ear plugs, now consigned to my helmet, hung from a nail within ready reach. With my footlocker still somewhere east of Suez, everything else stayed duffled.

Within its rim of cots, the squad room's only other furnishings were two of those big-armed student chairs positioned beneath a single bare 40-watt light bulb hanging halfway between my cot and the nearest exit onto the upstairs veranda. Those who would mend, manicure, read or write after dark waited in line to do so.

Our dining facility, located over a mile of calf-deep muck away, dispensed with seating altogether. Roomy enough to house the entire Ringling Brothers circus, man and beast – and just about as noisy – the mess served some 3,000 meals a day by minimizing menu choice and allowing only perpendicular eating at chest-high planks. On that first bracing walk back to barracks, I was still chewing my food.

Capt. Juanita Stryker, commanding, waited with her welcome: "You have been hand-picked," she said, "to come forward into a combat zone. This carries with it new responsibilities and dangers. There will be raids. Leave your helmet and shoes always near at hand.

"On red alert, extinguish all lights immediately, including cigarettes. If the warning is repeated, put on your combat gear and proceed without delay and in an orderly fashion to the dugout behind this building. Do not relax your vigilance or show any lights until the all clear sounds."

Already veterans of several weeks on location, my roommates didn't consider the enemy much of a threat. "Raids?" scoffed one. "Sure we have 'em. But mostly it's just Washing Machine Charlie paying a call. Easy to identify because his plane clanks like a Maytag in need of repair. Sneaks in before dawn under our radar, drops his 50 pounder, then hightails it for home. Hasn't hit anything important yet. But then, no one's hit him either."

Somewhat reassured, I bed checked for geckos, and prepared to retire. Which in those sweaty, sweltering climes meant shedding almost – if not – everything. To retain a modicum of modesty, I slipped into a tatty T-shirt whose hem hit me just below the navel, drifting off to sleep in bright moonlight to the antics of acrobatic geckos doing a high wire act on the beam above.

About 3 a.m. I faced one of life's more difficult decisions: whether to answer the call of my kidneys and make that backyard trek or force myself back to sleep and forget about it. Charlie settled the matter for me.

I half-heard his motor hiccoughing overhead; I sure as hell heard his bomb drop altogether too close. My father's earlier comments on my bravery under fire proved prophetic – I just wanted somewhere to hide. Under the cot wouldn't do – no crawl space. But the building itself, perched a possible two feet off the ground seemed a logical destination. What I didn't know was that Charlie was dropping a "daisy cutter" – an anti-personnel bomb which on impact sprayed lethal, low-level shrapnel in all directions. (It killed three of the bedridden wounded in the tent hospital behind us.)

Determined to save myself at all costs, I slammed on my helmet, foot powder blurring my vision, and raced for the porch – hitting those two rock-solid chairs in full flight, skidding belly-down all the way to the door. My knee caps quivering and quilled with splinters, I hobbled out to the head of the stairway while behind me indignant voices cursed the clown causing all the non-Charlie commotion.

Off to the side, Griffith leaned on the porch railing assessing the damage, and watched me emerge in the moon's spotlight. She couldn't miss me; I was the only one who bothered to get up.

"Really, Starbird," she said, "we've been damn tolerant about what you enlisted women wear. But don't you think you're carrying things a little too far?"

The Filipino sentry, grinning up from the foot of the stairs, evidentially didn't think so. Following his gaze, I realized that below the waist I was as bare as "September Morn." I could hear my mother saying "Don't worry, dear, you'll never see him again." Although he never saw quite as much of me again, he was still standing guard at the same spot when I left the area a month later.

Tucked above the local post office, our work space lay almost as far from our barracks as the consolidated mess – about a mile – but in the opposite direction. Trudging this water-logged triangle three times a day amid walling carabao, mired vehicles, and chicken-lugging citizens bound for a cock fight did a great deal for muscle tone, but damn little for dispositions.

Our one aging pair of field shoes never completely dried, we had no effective rain gear, and the starchiest laundress couldn't keep our clothes from crinkling up like seersucker once we stepped outside. (Except Griffith, of course – she rode.)

In fact, the clothes line between Washington and SWPA was still hopeless snarled. Especially for GHQ WACs who MacArthur, in refusing to accept them on permanent assignment, had set adrift on the seas of supply. We had yet to receive any suitable tropical issue, a supposed priority since before we arrived in Australia. When finally shipped, after a year of debate, most of it ended up everywhere in the Far East except where intended. Some transportation officers refused to carry items of WAC attire as being nonessential to the war effort with which, I'm sure, that grinning guard agreed.

The presence of local beauty shops in our new venue raised some hope for better grooming, but those brave enough to try them emerged after almost two hours under a hot helmet more frizzed than a New Guinea native, reeking strongly of ammonia and scorched hair.

Despite such cosmetic advancement and its role as provincial capital, Tacloban seemed little more than that average barrio with wanderlust, a scattered collection of single-story shops and elevated houses of palm and bamboo from which kids tumbled to cadge candy bars from GI Joe and Jane. Possibly among their number: a teenage hometown beauty named Meldy Romauldes who, later, as the profligate wife of Phillipine President Ferdinand Marcos, developed more extravagant tastes.

Missing from the scene: any Army-approved diversions, even the simple pleasures of Hollandia, where almost every camp at least offered open air movies almost every night. With nowhere to go but our own back porch, dating rules were modified: escorts need no longer arrive armed or accompanied by another couple, which circumstances provided in excess.

Some male officers fretted over our morale and health under such recreational limitations; even advocating sending us back to the high life in New Guinea for our own good. A poll taken at the time showed only 1 WAC in 100 would leave the area voluntarily – even to go home – until the war was won, and the job was done. Thanks to arm-twisters like Frink and Ginsburgh and the lack of anyone else to fill the expanding role WACs now played in the theater, we stayed.

In settling into our upstairs room, Griffith and I discovered that yet again females had not been factored into the Command's potty plans: the nearest facility belonged to an all-male map unit just across the street. Reaching it involved one of us sounding the alarm from our front window – "Coming through" – while the other bounded over some barely-buoyant duck boards, raced the length of a block yard building (amid shouts of encouragement along the way) and shot into the shed beyond, hoping someone had cleared the way. Dysentery days left no time for delays.

Such fanfare invariably attracted an audience of idling Filipinos – all sizes, both sexes – to the latrine's open doorway where they giggled and gabbed – probably over the absurdity of Americans insisting on a special place for this activity while for them all outdoors served as well.

Our back window faced a cluster of "split levels" – family on the top floor, pigs and chickens below; from this vantage point we observed a little of Leyte home life. Like mini-neighborhoods elsewhere on the island, this one shared a leafless backyard and a king-size cauldron – sort of a hot tub for hogs – in which and occasional porker was boiled alive to everyone's delight except the two "chickens" cringing with every squeal in the loft next door.

More precious than pig pots on the Tacloban scene and certainly more plentiful: the old treadle-type sewing machines, some dating from the turn of the century. Their presence in almost every household, where a single parachute would clothe an entire family, suggested that Issac Singer's peripatetic drummers hit the beach here about the same time Dewey routed the Spanish at Manila Bay.

Rain, almost a daily occurrence in that part of the world, continued to fall; commuting to meals grew more tedious with every trip. Adding to the irritation: a few hundred yards down the road and in full view of passersby, a small Ordinance group (30 to 40 men) dined in relative splendor, seated at tables, noshing away with obvious pleasure, and taking their time about it. Slogging past, I rather hoped they'd mistake me for an undernourished native on whom they regularly lavished their left-overs.

I certainly looked the part – mud-spattered, miserable, rain-soaked, wearing half a pup tent as a poncho. Even beneath this disguise, the mess crew finally recognized a fellow trooper (female) and invited me to join them. As of that moment, the consolidated mess and I parted company forever and I became a regular at their second seating when cadre and cooks were fed. For the duration of my stay in Tacloban, I happily chatted and chewed my way through the nearest thing to *cordon bleu* that SWPA had to offer.

Although the Ordinance mess drew substantially the same rations as every other (albeit in smaller quantities), its chefs were considerably more inspired, whipping powdered eggs that usually lie around in the only way they know how – scrambled – into frothy soufflés, quiches, and omelets with fold-in fillings that lent some flavor; elevating the dullest canned stew to a memorable *pot au feu* by liberally dousing it with their *vin de table*. Fermented from sugar, water, and every dried fruit available – prunes, figs, apples, apricots, raisins – it produced a moderately alcoholic beverage available at all meals including breakfast. These may not have been the most gung-ho warriors west of Truk but they sure were the happiest. Fortunately they were between engagements.

Jerry, self-appointed sommelier in faded fatigues and a sun-bright smile, ladled out my first cupful of this GI glüg with reassuring words: "I think madam will find this an unpretentious little wine – excellent nose – a taste both spritzy and crackling." A language Jerry learned as an apprentice vinter in upstate New York. "Note the eloquent lingering," he added, "the rich finish. This is indeed a vintage best drunk young." Which was well; given the demand, no batch lasted more than three days.

My assessment of its virtues fell a little short of Jerry's: a flavor much like sangria with its vague origins, and a bouquet right out of my grandfather's barn in cider season.

These Ordinance whizzes, experts with explosives, had

concocted something almost as lethal in their own backyard – by dripping their *vin de table* through a homemade still engineered from salvage plane parts, copper and brass scraps from shell casings. This Rube Goldberg contraption produced what they called "Tacloban tea" though TNT might have been more appropriate; it probably would have fueled a P-38 had anyone cared to try. Equally popular as an aperitif, mealtime grog, or after dinner drink – in fact, just about anytime – it occasionally flamed a *coq au vin* simmered from fallen gladiators of the cock-fight circuit, sinewy birds but at least not canned, cubed or dehydrated.

My diet improved appreciably, but with Frankie Filan off elsewhere, doing battle with his Leica, my wardrobe continued to disintegrate: fatigues stone-washed to filigree by the local laundry ladies; field shoes recently and quite badly resoled with slices of inner tube. But help was on the way – in the welcome form of George Champoux, a pre-war playmate who tracked me through my APO 500 number right to the schoolhouse door.

An old soldier once told me only three people in the Army were worth knowing: the sergeants three – mess, stable (now motor), and supply. George embodied the lot. Senior sergeant of Company C, 262nd Medical Evac Battalion on nearby Red Beach (where a bronze MacArthur still wades ashore to commemorate his landing) he had by week's end furnished me with a full set of oil skins, knee-high rubber boots, a Coleman stove, and the first of an uninterrupted stream of K rations from which I salvaged such usables as cheese, jelly, canned bacon, cigarettes, fruit bars, and tropical chocolate – the latter two to be consumed with caution since they had a way of speeding traffic through the alimentary canal.

It was good old George who introduced our back porch to the ice cream social, not only bringing in all the makings in three delicious flavors but also half his band of merry men to hand-crank the freezers through the tedious churning process.

Later George re-appeared with five former high-steel workers, Native Americans with sky-scraper credits, to patch the water tank so it would no longer hemorrhage our shower water above the halfway mark. Capering over roof and ridgepole, blow torches blazing, they not only earned our undying gratitude but also top billing as the best entertainment in town.

And it was George who rushed me off to his battalion dentist when I complained of a pinging bicuspid. Far removed from humorless hygienists, back issues of National Geographic, and an impressive investment portfolio, this doctor was definitely in – in a pyramidal tent, its sides rolled up for what little ventilation passed that way. Its interior, reduced to bare essentials, held a folding funeral chair permitting only a single patient position – rigidly upright – a drill apparatus powered by a treadle pedal and a lanky PFC named Harry, and – just out of reach – a number 10 can posing as a spit sink.

As most know, only two types of dentists exist in this world – hummers, and viewers-with-alarm who talk mostly in "tsks." My man, one of the former, made his own Muzak, endless emitting a throaty drone stuck on the first few bars of "Oh, What a Beautiful Morning." Although I had never considered dentistry a spectator sport, there, lolling around the periphery of our arena lay at least a company of the 262nd now on lunch break, mess kits in hand, waiting for the circus to begin.

Although Army dentists of the period, like those in Australia, preferred to pull, not patch, mine decided the damage was slight, a filling would do. He even primed me with a shot of GI alcohol in lieu of novacaine, altering my attitude somewhat but doing nothing to deaden the pain. Nor did Harry: after stomping the drill up to speed, he leaned into my mouth to monitor the action, completely forgetting his footwork to let the drill stutter slowly and agonizingly to a stop on a screaming nerve. The audience remained transfixed. The dentist hummed on.

A few weeks later, GHQ and all who toiled therein moved some fourteen miles down the road to Tolosa, a pre-war beach resort for Leyte's well-to-do. Fortunately, the relocation did nothing to imperil the Champoux connection, the distance to Red Beach being little more than from there to Tacloban.

The new site favored Michener's South Pacific over MacArthur's; our tented colony tucked amid chattering coconut palms, fronted Leyte Gulf whose water foamed a generous strip of bordering sand. Burlap barriers, which no one took seriously any longer, still separated the sexes – that is, female officers from the generals on one side, colonels on the other – with a well-beaten pass-through in between. And, as no surprise to anyone, officers separated enlisted from the view. My floorless, candlelit tent (down to 3 roommates) occupied the very back row, far removed form the siren song of the seas and inviting shoreline we were not permitted to visit except at inconvenient hours and fully clothed.

This travel-brochure setting plus one privilege Griffith managed to wrangle for me more than compensated for any deficit in scenic delights. Journalists billeted on Leyte shared with our commissioned PR personnel a splendid little mess close by the officers' cantonment area. The ultimate in SWPA sophistication, it offered such vaguely remembered refinements as hired waiters (paid for by its patrons), real butter that actually spread, ice water, and eggs which for the first time since Australia looked like God and the hen intended. By sneaking in and out before the subscribers, I dined so well for the next few weeks I put on three pounds and barely missed my Ordinance buddies. The stomach, on which an army is said to travel, seldom dwells on the past beyond the last meal.

Scarcely a dot on most maps, Toloso offered other advantages denied Tacloban: roads and pathways newly introduced to traffic heavier than plodding carabao remained relatively passable. And consolidating all our facilities at one consolidated location drastically reduced squishing about and virtually eliminated chaperoned sprints to the latrine.

One thing remained common to both places: rains continued to curtain the countryside, often roaring furiously through open-sided offices, spinning piles of paperwork into never-never land. Despite frantic retrieval efforts, most of this documentation sailed beyond recovery without causing the slightest blip in the war effort. Which should have told someone something – but never seemed to.

Somewhere within this time frame, Griffith (now a Captain) pulled off another minor miracle: she got me promoted to a T-5[12], sort of a clerical corporal. Naturally I enthused: "Two stripes!

---

12   The rank of T-5 stood for "Technician Fifth Grade," and was one rank above Private First Class, roughly equivalent to the rank of Corporal. Officially, technicians did not have the authority to give commands or issue orders, but in combat conditions they could be placed second in command of a squad by a Sergeant.

Wow! Sure going to make my sleeve look less lonesome. I don't want to seem ungrateful but wouldn't they have been more impressive without that dinky little 'T' under them?" Which I resented because it branded me as a typing type, not the line soldier I imagined myself.

"So," said Griffith, "next time I'll put you in for the Combat Infantry Badge."

This seemed an appropriate time to point out that, since ranking officers often pinned promotion insignia on commissioned subordinates (of which Griffith had none) she might do me the honor of sewing on my stripes. And dammed if she didn't, grudgingly of course, a favor she never let me forget for the next fifty-five years of her life.

Downpours continued unabated as did the office outpour of hometown releases that chronicled almost every move of every WAC in the entire Southwest Pacific area. To vary our task somewhat we did try to develop feature stuff that might quell any parental worries back home and send remaining daughters off to the recruiting station.

To make things look more appealing on the Far East front than they actually were (today they call it "spin") we sometimes dreamed up photo spreads of innocent sport between the sexes – days off together, beach picnics, softball games, sight-seeing, etc. – for which male models volunteered in droves. That is, until someone mentioned the same coverage would be distributed to their hometown papers as well.

They disappeared as the kids from Hamlin; our casting calls went unanswered: cavorting on sun-drenched beaches with a bevy of happy females hardly fit the grim tales of personal sacrifice and hardship transmitted in letters to mom, dad, and the girl(s) they left behind.

So back to promotions, transfers, and an occasional award – and coping with the mess and complications of carbon paper copies, the only duplication process then at our disposal. Such revolutionary advancements as the ditto copier and the mimeograph were available elsewhere – but not to us.

Fourteen

The Journey Home

"**D**ON'T GET too comfortable," Griffith cautioned one morning as she opened the mail (not an overwhelming job on our best day), "you're about to move again."

Manila at last!

By then our side had practically secured the city, pre-war "pearl of the Orient;" already POWs liberated from Los Banos and Santo Thomas University on February 3 and 4 had arrived in Tolosa on the first leg of their long journey home. Of them, the most remarkable to us were the 66 Army nurses taken off Corregidor when it fell in May 1942, and whose will and resilient spirit (both very much intact) had seen them through almost three years of Japanese captivity. Except for weight loss and dental neglect, they looked amazingly fit.

For their first R&R since war started, Leyte was certainly no Rue de la Paix. But we WACs, to them a new and baffling breed, did our best to ease the decompression process, divvying up our scarce cosmetics, clothing worn but still wearable (practically disrobing our dates in our enthusiasm), cigarettes, magazines (some not much newer than *Leslie's Illustrated Weekly*), and as the piece de resistance my mother's Vienna sausage! A little donated lipstick and a few bobby pins for hair control worked wonders for both their appearance and morale; in fact, they looked a hell of a lot better than we did. I even handed over my oilskins, Coleman stove, and bed pillow; it turned out I wasn't going to make it to Manila after all.

"As I was saying," continued Griffith, "you're on your way again. In fact, you may even beat those nurses home."

"Home? Whose dumb idea is that?"

"Yours!"

Having spent about 18 months as a very private soldier – buck and first class – the Army in its unfathomable wisdom decided a military career as promising as mine should not go unrewarded; I would again proceed without delay to Ft. Des Moines (déjà vu) to join the 57th Officers' candidate class. That application for OCS, submitted at a low period six months earlier, had finally settled my fate.

"Aw, c'mon m'am. I don't want to go. Certainly we can negotiate."

"Corporal, you're going. I know what would happen when we go up North: things get a little rough and you'd be moaning 'what am I doing in this hole when I could be fat-catting it back in the States?' No way am I going to listen to that."

"But who's going to gofer all those goodies to which you have become accustomed?"

"No sweat, Corporal. Sergeant Champoux has kindly agreed that, if I get him a date with your replacement, I shall not want. All we're doing is removing a link from the chain of supply."

"Traitors! Both of you!"

I went, of course – missing to this day having missed Manila. Griffith was right about one thing – the WACs tour there was no cake walk. Enemy resistance ended on March 4; the first WACs moved in three days later to a city in ruins and probably the worst living and working conditions encountered by any WAC anywhere. Here they would remain, illness and exhaustion depleting their numbers, until all hostilities ceased in August, unofficial V - J Day when the War Department ordered those remaining to return home ASAP, a move that took until January '46 to complete. Hanging around for the occupation of Japan was not an option, though some returned as DACs – Department of the Army civilians – almost immediately.

As for my own departure, it proceeded with as much delay as possible: to Tacloban for a final "tea" with the boom-boom boys; to Red Beach for more of the red carpet treatment; a last evening in town which segued right through curfew to pre-dawn take-off during which we toasted my health so vigorously I had little left. George and company stayed with me to the bitter end, boosting me aboard a DC-4 with a box lunch as big as a bathtub, which I used to barter my way onto the crew's flight deck bunk with its restorative oxygen supply.

Fellow passengers for the run to Guam included Harvey, an Air WAC staff sergeant also headed for OCS, and forty Marine pilots, all Chippendale look-alikes, being rotated home. As I tacked forward for some sleep time, I heard Harvey agree to sit in for a few friendly hands of poker, at which she was a closet whiz. When I returned after a 2-hour nap, she was $400 ahead but rapidly losing it in a crap shoot about which she knew almost nothing. So it went for both Harvey and her fortunes as we crossed the Southwest Pacific – up at cards, down at dice – until she debarked with a surprising $523 in winnings. If the Marines expected to get Harvey back on her knees to recoup their losses on the continuing trip to San Francisco, wrong! Being among the lowest on the military totem pole, we were bounced off the flight – over their loud protests, they were not.

Our enforced layover proved extremely pleasurable; it not only preserved Harvey's cache of cash, someone thoughtfully provided us with two cheery escorts with whom we leisurely toured the island, did some overdue beach time, got mobbed at the NCO club as the first non-patient to pass through, and stocked up at every mess hall which served whatever the hour. At the first of these, I consumed eleven eggs – every way but scrambled; Harvey downed two quarts of ice cream in four different flavors. Even the kitchen staff watched and applauded.

This photo ran with the following caption in the Hamilton Field paper on March 3, 1945: "A milk run on the Post Exchange was the first idea that Cpl Ethel Starbird had when she got in from the Philippines. She couldn't even wait to sit at a table, but started drinking milk and eating scoops of ice cream at the counter."
(Photo by the Hamilton Field Base Laboratory)

I felt we certainly owed someone thanks for all this hospitality, but who? Somehow the headquarters of Millard F. Harmon, head of the Strategic Air Command in Guam and concurrently Deputy Commander, 20th Air Force, which we were then passing through, seemed a likely spot. And the General's aide, at hand when I entered, seemed a likely person. While I was expressing our appreciation, the General himself drifted out of his office, took a double take at what the war had washed up on his doorstep, and said "I recognize the stripes, Corporal, but not the uniform. Just what army do you represent?"

Even at ram-rod attention, everything on me drooped – and although our government had issued every item I wore to someone, not even a three-star general could identify their origins. Perhaps to satisfy his curiosity and to get a better fix on my service status, the General asked me to tea. Sipping Darjeeling in china cups, I mentioned that as much as we enjoyed the stopover, it had eliminated any chance of my getting to my home in Vermont for even a brief delay en route before reporting to Des Moines.

"Maybe I can help out," said the General. "I'm heading for Washington later this afternoon – straight through – with only a few quick refueling stops en route. I could drop you on the East Coast before you can catch a plane out of here. At least give you time to say 'hello' to your folks." A delightful prospect and extremely generous offer, but one I had to refuse: his plane had room for only one more passenger and Harvey and I were traveling on the same set of orders to San Francisco where new ones to new destinations would have to be cut. And getting out of Burlington on a fast turn-around was certainly iffy.

By the time Harvey and I reached Kwajalein late the following night, Harmon's plane and all aboard had vanished into the sea somewhere between Johnston Island and Honolulu; no trace was ever found.

Arriving and departing Kwaj in total darkness limited our view of the atoll (which would hardly excite enthusiasm) to yet another mess hall open round the clock to feed airmen, ground crews, and transients like us. This time we disappointed the duty staff; they were expecting far more distinguished visitors – the first wave of

Corregidor nurses who, after our goofing off on Guam, were only a few hours behind us.

As we fortified ourselves for the hop to Johnston, a flour-dusted cook loomed over our table. Tall, gangly, he looked like Gary Cooper playing Sgt. York pulling KP. Toe-scuffing shy, he asked if I would come out to the supply room with him, he had something to show me. Now, that's the kind of proposition that can get a girl in trouble.

I went anyway.

There, on a makeshift table of barrels and boards lay his masterpiece: a cake roughly the dimensions of a queen-size mattress bearing a frothy frosting message: "Welcome Home You Wonderful Women." For the sake of the beaming baker and others like me who shared his sentiments, I could only hope the nurses stopped long enough to read what he had written.

Whether or not, they reached California's Hamilton Field, just north of San Francisco, the day after we did – where their welcome at their own request was confined to family, invited friends, and by special dispensation, Harvey and me. Those truly wonderful women walked off that plane as buoyant as holiday-makers: the only comment I heard from that quarter "Give us a chance to fatten up a little and you bet we're going back."

Since paperwork and getting tarted up in new winter uniforms trapped us at Hamilton for another two days, Harvey and I felt we owed ourselves at least one night on a highly touted town whose only attractions we had seen outbound were Alcatraz, Coit Tower and the Golden Gate Bridge.

Wartime San Francisco was a mob scene, albeit a high-spirited one; sooner or later just about everyone from everywhere stopped by. With me in tow, Harvey plunged into a queued up crowd milling around a night club featuring Sophie Tucker playing, for the fifth year, her farewell performance.

"C'mon, Harve," I bellowed, "we'll never get in here. Let's try someplace else."

"Don't fret. Just follow me." Then, chanting "friend of Miss Tucker's, friend of Miss Tucker's" she elbowed us right into the lobby and the arms of the club owner whom she reminded (true or not) of their earlier acquaintance when she worked for the

Los Angeles Daily News. He was also impressed, no doubt, by her broken field running and her combat stars, still a rare sight among WAC returnees. He seated us Tucker-side where the well-rounded chanteuse joined us between sets to laud our patriotism – and our appetites.

As guests of the management, we both ordered our dream re-entry dinner: shrimp cocktail, filet mignon, baked potato erupting with sour cream and for me the largest artichoke from Monterey fields. As a suitable accompaniment, we chose a quick succession of martinis which after over a year's abstinence had an extremely forceful and cheering effect.

Somewhere between appetizer and entrée, Harvey – less experienced than I with the punch martinis packed – toddled off to a phone booth in the ladies' room to inform her family in Los Angeles of her homecoming, while I went along scarffing down food and drink, even her share when she failed to return. Just before dessert I decided Harvey had been talking long enough, it was my turn to call home.

In a manner of speaking, she was still on the phone, slumped on the floor fast asleep, the ear piece still in her hand.

As I was rearranging her on the chaise (this being a posh place) two WAC officers came barreling in. Harvey was in no condition to stand up and salute.

"Is she sick?" one asked.

"Or drunk?" sniffed the other.

"Please, ma'm, certainly not that," I said looking as offended as possible. "It's more like battle fatigue." I turned Harvey ever so slightly so her battle stars showed. "Notice her yellow color: advanced jaundice." I felt her forehead. "Getting feverish; probably a malaria attack coming on. They're pretty rough to watch. You may want to leave before it happens." Leprosy, my next diagnosis had it been necessary, could not have stampeded the Gold Bar Twins out of there any faster; they had no intention of ruining an evening with Sophie Tucker with an evening tending two diseased enlisted women.

Now it was my turn to touch base with the folks back home. Forgetting it was 4 a.m. back on the East Coast, I rang the family's six-party line, the only phone service available to them when they moved to the farm in 1942.

My father answered: "Yes. Hello. Who n'hell's calling at this ungodly hour?"

"Your warrior daughter, Dad. Old Pallas Athena herself. How's the weather back there?"

"Forget the weather; figure it any way you want to – this is Vermont. You don't sound like you're in the Philippines – you know that's where your mother and I met. Just where are you anyway?"

"San Francisco."

I heard mother's disembodied voice commenting from the wings: "Alfred, do watch your language. Remember the neighbors."

He was remembering them all right. The same rings that called him to the phone woke up the five other subscribers on the same circuit. Too early for milking, too late to go back to sleep, they stayed on the line to find out what the pre-dawn disturbance was all about. Each one cutting in further faded our transcontinental connection until dad's voice (and I assume mine too) was barely a whisper.

Dad bellowed at the local switchboard operator whose only employment enjoyment came from listening in. "Mary, dammit, Mary! I know you're awake. Tell those damn fools to hang up. And fast. This is my daughter just back from the Pacific and I want to talk to her. There's a war out there, y'know? Besides, they'll hear all about it tomorrow at the Post Office anyway." A series of sign-off clicks restored the service to full power.

At last, dad came through loud and clear: "What'd they send you home for?"

"Officer Candidate School."

"And you agreed?"

"Hey, I thought you'd be pleased. Besides, it didn't look like I'd ever make sergeant." Staff Sergeant being the only rank I truly coveted.

"So what's your rank now?"

"T-5"

"T-what? What in holy hell is a T-5?" My father's intimacy with Army minutiae ceased in 1930.

"A sort of Corporal."

"And you're giving that up? It's the best rating in the Army. Nobody notices you too much and if a Sergeant gives you something to do you don't like you can always fob it off onto some poor private. You get to be a Second Lieutenant you're back at the bottom again, shoveling out the stables – so to speak."

Having risen through the ranks himself from enlisted volunteer in 1898 to Brigadier General in World War I, I figured my father should know what he was talking about.[13]

He did.

---

13   Starbird's father, Alfred Andrews Starbird, enlisted in the 1st Maine Infantry for the Spanish American War on May 13, 1989. He was commissioned a Second Lieutenant of Artillery in the Regular Army on July 9, 1898, and served through various grades to Brigadier General. He retired from the Army at his own request, after more than thirty years of service, on February 6, 1930.

Afterword

S O THE reader will not think my meteoric rise in the Army was due to my father's influence and rank: of the first, he had none – and of the second, nothing in my official records showed his occupation as anything but "retired farmer."

I entered the Service determined to advance strictly on my own merit.

Given the results achieved[14], I did.

---

14   Starbird's brief career in the Women's Army Corps, which started with her volunteer enlistment as a Private in 1943, ended honorably in 1945 as a commissioned Second Lieutenant.

Headed for OCS, Two WACs from Philippines Stop Over Here, Tell of Overseas Life

Hamilton Field Paper
March 3, 1945

The tables are turned, in this story, on two WACs who, for the last three months have been the writers rather than the subjects of newspaper articles: S/Sgt Ruth Harvey and T/5 Ethel Starbird, who arrived here last week from the Philippine Islands, on their way to OCS at Ft. Des Moines, Iowa.

Like any GIs returning to the states after almost a year's absence, the WACs wanted a hot bath, fresh eggs, quarts of milk, and a look at San Francisco after phoning home. But they took time out to sit on the other side of the reporter's desk for an hour and spin tales and reminisce about GI life and WAC doings in the Southwest Pacific Theatre.

The girls flew into Hamilton Field from the Philippines, wearing the suntan slacks that are regulation out there. At debarkation, they received OD's, shirts, low cut shoes, and they hurried to the PX to buy their first Philippine Liberation ribbons.

Both Sgt. Harvey and Cpl. Starbird have been gone almost a year, and just before they came home, were in public relations work.

Ruth was in the first WAC group to go down under, the first outfit to go into tents in Guinea, and was herself the first enlisted WAC to arrive in Hollandia, as secretary to the Chief of Staff of the Far East Air Force. Both girls have been in Australia, New Guinea, and the Philippines, and their excitement over their return home is tempered by the fact that they personally didn't get to Manila before they left.

In Brisbane they lived in huts in mid-winter, with no heat and no plumbing; in Hollandia in tents, and in the Philippines in a former mission school.

'Life for the WACs overseas is just as it is for the men, where we were," Ethel says. 'We live, eat and sleep the same way the GI's do. No special privileges. But the men themselves treat us like queens. They build our furniture, decorate our dayroom, do everything they can for us."

The WACs don't have any easy time overseas and the jobs certainly can't be considered glamorous, the sergeant says. 'All the WACs work hard and long. I was at my office every day, seven days a week, from 7:30 a.m. to 11 p.m. many days,' she added.

The offices were furnished with packing crates as desks and filing cabinets; portable typewriters, and benches, if anything, left behind by the Japanese.

GI ingenuity overseas isn't the monopoly of the men, the two WACs aver. The girls made dressing tables out of crates and covered them with hand painted burlap; stuck their candles in hollowed coconut shells; and made hangers out of odd pieces of wire.

Ethel says that "we went into pants when we got to Guinea and as you can se we were still in them when we landed here. We ate dehydrated foods out of mess kits. We washed in helmets and drank from Lister bags. We laundered our clothes in long troughs, hanging them in the sun to dry and hoping they wouldn't fall into the Guinea dust or Philippine ankle-deep mud; and pressed them between the blankets that served as mattresses on our cots. Sure I want to go back again, and I hope I can," she added laughingly but seriously.

Ethel's home is in Burlington, Vt., where she worked as a copywriter for an advertising agency. Ruth is from Los Angeles where she was secretary to the managing editor of the Los Angeles Daily News and did free-lance writing on the side. The two girls met in Brisbane when they pulled KP together. Ethel was attached to General headquarters of the United States Armed Forces in the Far East; and Ruth to the Far East Air Force.

From the Hamilton Field Paper, March 3, 1945. (Hamilton Field, California). Used by permission.

Seven WACs Proud of Service Ribbons and Atabrine Tint

Mt. Pleasant News
April 27, 1945; p. 5

Fort Des Moines, Iowa (INS) – Seven WACs attending officers candidate school at Fort Des Moines pointed with pride today to their service ribbons and atabrine tint. The seven voted unanimously in favor of returning overseas after receiving their hard-earned gold bars.

They were among the first WACs to set foot in Australia and were among the first detachment in New Guinea, known as the "New Guinea Pigs" because of the experimental nature of their job. Four ventured into the Philippines on the heels of the dough-boys still smashing the Japs from Leyte.

"We toiled and sweat, griped and groaned, slogged through the mud – and loved every minute of it," they agreed.

The officer candidates returned from the Pacific area to Fort Des Moines for further training are: Ruth Harvey, New York, N.Y., and formerly of the Daily News in Los Angeles, Calif.; Ethel A. Starbird, Underhill, Vt.; Barbara Dement, Walnut Creek, Calif.; Lena Morton, Washington Ind.; Alice Cleydon, Fredonia, N.Y.; Thelma Boyer, Hemmatite, Mo.; and Dorothy Starr, Carmel, N.Y.

Candidate Boyer was the first enlisted woman to step from the large army transport plane bearing the advance group of WACs to New Guinea.

The "New Guinea Pigs" claimed the toughest job of WACs in the South Pacific. Their ability to adapt themselves to the tropics would decide if the women soldiers would advance further into the jungles or fall back to Australia. They were successful, and today they were proud of their job, their ribbons and the yellowish color of their skin caused by the atabrine used to ward off malaria.

From The Mount Pleasant News, April 27, 1945. (Mt. Pleasant, Iowa). Used by permission.

Ethel A. Starbird was commissioned as a Second Lieutenant on March 5, 1945.

Travel Journalist Saw the World With Humor, Curiosity and Guts

By Matt Schudel
Washington Post Staff WriterSunday, August 14, 2005; C10

L ong after she had retired, Ethel Starbird lingered in spirit at the National Geographic. From 1961 to 1983, she was a writer and editor with the magazine, traveling the globe as one its few female staff writers.

She wrote articles on Hawaii, Saskatchewan, England's Thames River, the islands of Spain and her beloved New England. Each of them required months and sometimes years of research, travel, writing and polishing.

For a story on coffee in the magazine's March 1981 issue, Starbird worked for more than two years, picking coffee beans in the mountains of Colombia, searching for authentic Turkish coffee in Istanbul and visiting plantations in Brazil and the Ivory Coast. In Japan, she was buried up to her neck in a therapeutic bath of coffee grounds heated to 140 degrees. In Indonesia, a coffee farmer told her of a prized local variety made from beans digested in the belly of a small animal called the luak.

"He refilled my cup," she wrote in her article. " 'I'd like to try it sometime,' I told him more out of politeness than conviction.

" 'You just did.' "

Ethel Allan Starbird, who died June 27 of a stroke at age 87, was admired not just for her writing but for her straight-shooting personality, her love of a good time and her willingness to stand up to cant and nonsense. Her career had taken her from the military to radio to politics, but at the Geographic, she wrote in an unpublished memoir, she found "the most civilized place in Washington to work."

She was so beloved that, for years, the magazine presented an annual award called "the Ethel" to a writer, editor or researcher who best embodied what her colleagues called her spirit of "integrity, good humor and guts."

If the pages of her articles have begun to fade, the impression she made on others has not.

"She was smart, funny, generous, as well as stubborn, opinionated and sometimes mercurial," former colleague Betsy Moize said.

"She was abrasive as all get out and cantankerous," said writer Bart McDowell, "but also a very loyal and feisty person."

"If a woman could be a curmudgeon," said Geographic researcher Judith Brown, "she was a curmudgeon."

Starbird was born in Washington but spent most of her youth in Vermont, graduating in 1938 from the University of Vermont. Her father and her brother were Army generals, and Starbird herself served two years in the Women's Army Corps during World War II.

Her official job, she said, was preparing news releases, but her unofficial duty was writing Dear John letters for other women in her unit, which she called "some of the most creative work I have ever done."

Posted to war zones in the Pacific theater, she wrote in her memoirs, she didn't always observe strict military decorum and sometimes found herself wearing, "all at the same time, a Navy overseas cap, Marine shirt, Seabee dungarees, Air Corps jacket and jungle boots courtesy of the Japanese Imperial Army."

From 1945 to 1951, Starbird worked in radio and advertising in Burlington, Vt., Honolulu, San

Francisco and Tokyo before joining Dwight D. Eisenhower's 1952 presidential campaign. By the end of the year, she was assistant to the chairman of the Republican National Committee, in charge of coordinating women's activities. She worked for the U.S. Information Agency and the General Services Administration before signing on with the Geographic as a writer of "legends," or photo captions.

The magazine had its share of traditions and, as Starbird discovered, secrets. Finding an office with a constantly closed door, she decided to investigate, "which is how, after seven years of clandestine operation, I managed to blow the cover on the conspiracy within -- the FBI's 24-hour vigilance from the Geo's garret on the Russian Embassy across the street."

Gregarious and generous, Starbird always followed an open-door policy in her own office, especially as the clock approached 5 p.m.

"She would invite people in for a 'smile,' as she said," McDowell recalled, "which was her Inver House Scotch Whisky and general gossip."

She had scores of friends, whom she invited to her weekend house on the Rappahannock River for an annual "summer camp," complete with printed T-shirts, contests and a schedule for kitchen duty. Dozens of people came to her weekend-long parties that invariably devolved into discordant concerts on the kazoos, tambourines, penny whistles and broomstick bass she kept on hand.

The best party of all, though, came in 1978, for her 60th birthday. After a five-course meal, Starbird led the revelers on a frolic through the ornamental pool in the Geographic's ground-floor Explorers Hall, as perplexed tourists peered through the windows.

That year, her friends pitched in to buy her a full set of drums -- just the thing for someone who marched to no one's drumbeat but her own.

Starbird at her drums in her apartment at The Fairfax. Ft. Belvoir, Virginia, 1988.
(Photo by Susan Starbird Stout)